Drowning

By
Clarence Kenny Plank

Table of Contents:

About this book:

When I started writing my seventh book "Death of A Gentlemen" I figured that would be my last book of poetry I would do. I got burned out from life, which is something everyone goes through at some point in their life, when you just get tired of everything. You get tired of fighting for things that seem pointless in the grand scheme of things. I lost my friend last year. She was my number one fan, and that lost affected me more than any other. I guess after awhile you get frustrated from losing people, things, or yourself at times. She was a beautiful soul. We hung out a few times together, sometimes for hours, just talking. We chatted more on social media, and she always loved my poetry. It wasn't just her though that made me lose heart. No matter what I did, my books weren't selling, and doing spoken word poetry became frustrating to perform when people didn't care. It became evident every time I took the stage. I worked on reading the room, but no one wants to hear about love. How can you speak of to a society who doesn't know the meaning of it? After taking some time off and looking to take things in a different direction in my writing in publishing an actual book. I've started and rewrote the beginning of that book a bunch of times before walking away from it.

It took me sometime to get over my friend, who I miss, just like all the other people who have left this life.

That brings me to this book. Whenever I'm writing a poetry book, I create a cut off point, where I edit the book and any other poems I happen to make are moved to another document for the next book. These are the poems I have strung together using word prompts, music, T.V. series or movies, where I had found a spark of inspiration. There was a time when I had a series crush on two different women who sparked some of the words written in the text. In their own way they were beautiful, and in that moment I was misplaced for a time in wanting to hold onto a woman, deep down in my soul. I knew I could never be with. I guess we all have those people, we aren't meant for because something about us doesn't mesh well with them. It is what it is. Most people may have read these poems on my Instagram account or Facebook, but I've only posted half of the poem on those sites, so you get a real treat in being the only person who will know the meaning of a certain poem, while others with not.

Contact information:
Instagram: @Nitejokertn
Twitter: @nitejoker
Youtube: @Shoeboxpoet
Facebook: @theshoeboxpoet45
Facebook: @Nitejoker
Tik-Tok: @kennyplank
www.shoeboxpoet.com

Books:
"Finding Peace Within the Storm"
"The Shoebox Poet"
"Writer of Wrongs"
"Poems From A Heart Shaped Box"
"Words For A Muse"
"Words Beneath Her Skin"
"Death Of A Gentleman"

Freely
With her obsidian crown,
She was fearless,
In how she found,
The courage,
To take back her life,
From the clutches,
Of her captor.
She learned to breathe freely again.

Stained
Angels are fearless,
While demons,
Carry hearts of obsidian,
Incased in horrors.
She was a rarity,
Being the only angel,
Who loved with a black heart,
Made of stained glass.

Fall
Those memories,
Fall in the rain drops,
Blue ghosts in the rain,
Of you and me.

Along with other memories,
Of other lovers,
The oceans' tears gathered,
On the winds of

◆ ◆ ◆

Sheets
I awoke,
And rubbed,
My dreary eyes.
As I found us,
Entangled,
In a net of limbs,
Covers and sheets.
It was mixed exposure,
Of the night's cool,
And your body heat,
Draped in sweat.
Intertwined,
Like a couple of bugs,
Is a spider's web.
Just you and I,
Rising with the morning sun.
You stretched,
Reaching for fading stars,
Of the night.
Our eyes met,
And your smile,
Was radiant,
In the dawn's early light,
And all I wanted to do,
Was remain here,
With you.

◆ ◆ ◆

Sky

Sparkling eyes,
Of sky blue,
Peaceful sleep.
Waken to my touch,
A smile,
As I gaze,
Into the heavens,
Of a thousand stars,
In the vast cosmos,
Of your soul.
And here I sit,
Mesmerized,
By the glow,
Of the star,
Burning,
Behind those eyes.

❖ ❖ ❖

Marrow

He's a cunning man,
Who preys upon the weak,
And you are his target.
He will devour you,
Not in the way you want,
With seduction,
Or passion,
But with deceit,
As he rips your heart,
From your chest,
As he sucks your soul,
From your marrow,
And bones.

❖ ❖ ❖

Celestial bodies
Lie covered,
In a blanket of stars,
And morning dew.
Distracted,
By the moment,
As two lovers,
Get lost,
In the throes of spring,
While bathing,
In a sublime sunrise.

Foolish days of spring
Being lost in the moments,
Of our youth.
Those days,
Where innocence,
Of days watching clouds,
Drift by in a nearly still,
Summer's breeze.
Beads of sweat,
Drape your face,
After playing,
For hours,
Under a streetlight's glow,
And the dance of lightning

Recalling
Far and here,
Is my thoughts,
Have been of late.

Where I recall,
The memory,
Of my love for you.

◆ ◆ ◆

Bare
Whispering words,
That only you,
Can me speak.
Whispering voices,
Of meaningful words,
In the darkness,
Where we can,
Be ourselves,
Laid bare.
Naked like a candle's flame.

◆ ◆ ◆

Dream of blossoms
You have to dig deep sometimes,
And trust the vision of your soul,
If you want to grasp your dreams,
And hold them in your arms.
That's why the poet in me bloomed,
When I made the choice,
To write words about,
Blushing blossoms,
And the cradle of rain drops,
After April showers,
Fill them.
Being in the lost valley,
Of the imagination,
In wrapping my arms,
Around your body.

And the dreams,
That rise and fall,
In my mind over and over again.
When I wish to taste your lips,
As staring at your photograph,
For hours after our conversations.
It's this trust I placed in stardust,
To lead me back to the collect atoms,
Of a heavenly goddess.
Whose red lips,
I have longed to kiss,
And touch the amulet,
Of your heart,
With my fingertips,
While you leave,
Your fingerprints,
One my heart and soul.

❖ ❖ ❖

Severed ties
And lies,
That slowly dies,
From the disconnection,
Of your parted lips,
And sipping the drug,
Of your mindless fears.
Being unbound,
And hounded,
From the madness,
Of your dreamless sleep

❖ ❖ ❖

I built a shrine
To the beauty,

Of you.
Where I worshiped you,
Like a goddess.
A shrine,
Where my tears,
Were the offering,
For all those times,
In longing,
To be the one,
Who kisses your lips,
Holds you close,
And feels your body shake,
When we make love.
I've shed more tears,
And collected them,
But I stand to reason,
If those tears are mixed,
With the blood stains,
Of all the times,
I've had to sacrifice,
My life just to exist,
In your world.

Sound of fire
My inspiration,
When night falls,
And we settle in,
To the sound of,
Of a fire,
And I kiss,
Her velvet lips.
With every touch,
Between us,
I record those seconds,

Of drinking in her skin,
With my touch,
As I piece together,
The lines of your naked,
Body in my arms.

Grounding yourself
Your dainty feet,
Played in the grass,
When we walked,
In the meadow.
You took off your shoes,
To let the clovers,
And wildflowers,
Gently caress them.
Bare feet in the grass,
Was a lovely feeling,
For a child of nature,
Like you.
Grounding yourself,
After a stressful week.
As you picked flowers,
Pinching them,
Between your toes,
While we laid in a blanket,
Of wildflowers,
That danced over us,
In the breeze.
You played with flowers,
While I messed with your hair,
Running my fingers,
Through those golden locks.

I awoke to a familiar sound
The one where,
You know you're not alone.
It was a melancholy song,
Playing a phantom tune of a piano.
You played that tune,
A thousand times,
To our children,
Who grew in your arms,
And you taught them,
Those same chords,
That play in the stillness,
Of the night.

◆ ◆ ◆

Amateur
Does he fan the flames,
Of love for you?
Or was it lust all the way?
He's a project in the making,
A rebuild of rehabilitation,
For an expert like you,
An amateur psychologist,
With the means to fan the sparks,
So, he will catch fire,
And become a better man?
Alas,
You're playing with fire,
When he breaks your heart,
Knocks you up,
And leaves you dime less,
Because inflation makes,
Pennies and people useless.
You knew better,

But you have the power,
To undo it all with your love,
Because boring guys,
Are a waste of time,
When you have someone,
Who works his hustle,
For cash and a cause,
While you making ends meet,
Taking care of things,
And starving babes,
Or let them slide.
Meanwhile,
Hubby is out,
Spreading lies,
And spreading thighs,
Working his angle,
Along with his dangle.
It don't matter,
When you found a way,
To keep his dreams ablaze,
While you can't afford a cream,
To stop that flaming itch,
In your divide.

Song of madness
What is it that's so fascinating about you?
I want to believe you're evil,
In how you are a Mozart of heartstrings,
When you pluck them without a cause.
You always leave me broken,
With your smile and alluring eyes.
And I die every time you play those cords.

Short verse
Some call me the Mozart of heartstrings,
In how I can pluck every string,
With a short verse or two.
It's not science,
Because we've all been there,
One way or another,
Dying,
When we hang on their every word,
Wishing they would give in, comeback,
Or never left us.

◆ ◆ ◆

Living life in storms.
You learn how to live.
How the raindrops become kisses,
When the storm rages against you.

◆ ◆ ◆

Findings
This is how I feel,
Not who I am.
Let my words,
Unfold my emotions,
So, they can draw you in.
When those storms,
And raindrops,
Come rolling in,
On the distant horizon.
Let me take you someplace,
Other than being here.
A place where you can escape,
And dwell in other emotions,

Of pleasant memories,
When you reminisce,
About those days,
When you could smile,
Laugh and love,
Without being hesitant,
Where I lead you,
To understanding yourself,
And find hope where you left it,
Inside of you.

You're beautiful
In whom you are,
So much so,
Women would kill,
To have your curves,
Because they're the definition,
Of the sculpture of a goddess.
Those stretch marks,
There are things,
Some women long for,
In bringing life,
Into the world,
And understand,
The meaning,
Of being a mother.
The beauty of your spirit,
Cloaked in the magic of love.

How many soft whispers
Did I call to you,
From the void?

Just so I our love,
Would bloom,
Across the distance,
Of time and space.
Faint echoes coursing,
Through the cosmos,
To reaching out,
To the piece of your soul,
You want her more.

Pic-4
She drug me from the train,
Leading me by the hand,
Along the winding path.
She was excited to see me,
She was lovely,
As she moved through,
The streets to her place.
Once behind closed doors,
We kissed, soft and deep.

She stared out
The world through my window,
At the people below.
Until a bird landed,
The feline became curious.

Falling grains of sand
Through the hourglass,
Every grain was a time,

I made love to you,
Died in your arms,
And at times,
I became you,
And you, me.
With every breath,
I took between kisses,
And hazy dreams,
Of waking up next to you.
You came into my life,
Leaving my heart ajar,
With every passing grain,
Of sand flowing,
Through my glass heart.

You call it an illness
I call it my reality,
When it comes,
To my mental health.
From the prescriptions,
I take,
Just to balance the pain inside,
From the words,
Echoing through my head.
The drugs I take,
To help me react,
And think in a world,
That dismisses me,
Even when I act normal.
It's a constant thing,
Of finding my worth,
Within myself,
Even if the world,
May not show me,

I deserve so much more.
You give me drugs,
To right the chemicals,
That swirl around in my brain,
Sometimes,
Silencing the only voice,
Of reason to play out,
The unnormal things,
Which cloud my head.
Thoughts,
Of sex,
Money,
Fun,
And poetry.
When my thoughts run dry.
Thoughts,
Dreams and loves.
Then the dam breaks,
When the drugs effect end,
And I have to face,
The raging monster,
Of anxiety and depression,
Alone.

◆ ◆ ◆

It's a flawed design
When it comes,
To Imagining,
What loving you,
Would be like,
Beyond our destiny,
Where loving the cosmos,
Deep within you.

◆ ◆ ◆

Fallen
Blank verses,
Hidden among the pages,
Where I once lingered.
It haunts me.
How you turned the pages,
Of my heart with your fingers.
Listening to every word,
Every syllable spoken,
From your velvet lips.
The ache of saudade,
And the things I long to remember,
About the way your fingers felt.
Even though the pain I felt,
From your pen,
The words and your touch,
Soothed the wounds,
And healed my scars.
I regret this taste of solitude,
As I lay here.
Dreaming of your face,
Gathering covers,
Just to imagine you,
Lying next to me again.

I used to journal
All the details,
Of my dreams,
Inscribing dreams,
All the crazy things,
That enter my mind,
As I slept,
Sometimes,

Dreaming of you.
While other times,
It's a jumble of stories,
Of fears, hopes and desire.
In wanting so much more,
And feeling defeated.

You're my secret
Lost in the moonlit dream,
Of your kisses.
From the mountains,
To distant peaks,
Across deep oceans,
Just to gaze,
Upon your face,
For one last time.

Hill of stones
As far as the eye,
Can see to the distance.
She places stones.
As she moves on with her life.

She gathered a hill of stones
Clutching in her hand,
Before releasing one,
Skipping,
Across a plain of glass.
As ripples dance,
On the surface.

❖ ❖ ❖

She thought about the new beginning
She was anxious to share with him,
Only to let the memory fade.

❖ ❖ ❖

You used to believe
He hung and painted stars,
Just for you.
A crooked moon,
He gave you.
It was a sad feeling,
When he left you,
As you tried to wipe away,
The fingerprints,
That lined your heart.
They were a reminder,
Of how he tasted,
On your lips.
All the memories,
That roll through,
The darkness of your head.
All of those times,
You kissed him,
In the rain,
Where those same rain drops,
Wash away the tears,
You shed in silence.
Just to forget his touch,
But it all comes crashing,
Down like some tide,
When you catch his scent,
On the air,

Or in your bed.
You want to walk,
Back into his life,
Only goodbyes are harder,
When,
He's standing at the altar,
Without you.
You say, "Still I rise,"
Only to fall back,
Into those memories,
Of wanting a lover,
Who walked away,
From all you had,
Because he wanted more,
Than you could give,
Other than your heart.

Collage of hearts
He collected
A collage of hearts,
Searching for the one,
Who's heartbeat,
Matched his,
To no avail,
He change his rhythm,
To match hers,
And found himself,
Dying in the arms,
Of a beauty,
Who's erratic beat,
Sustained his life.

Eyes sing of sorrow
Of a soul yearning,
To break free,
Of the shackles,
Holding her back,
From spreading,
Her gossamer wings,
Of thread, woven lace,
And blues.
She's like grains of sand,
Shifting through the hourglass,
Riding waves of satin,
Making dreams,
Of a mystique beauty,
Come to life.
With the touch of her hands,
And the warmth of her skin.
Outstretched arms,
Welcome tired souls,
For a lover's embrace.
Tasting her lips,
A divine wine,
Laced with passion,
And merlot.
A bittersweet,
Connection,
Tasting smoky wine,
Of embers in her kiss.
As you trace the jewels,
Of her back with your fingertips.

◆ ◆ ◆

Every
Line.

I
Fall
Deeper
Into
You.
So,
Far
I
Can't
Feel
Myself
Anymore.
Even
When
I
Breathe
You
In.

Dancing red flags
It was chaos,
Falling recklessly,
For you.
But I was hooked,
By the mystery,
And magic,
Of your gaze.
I was set,
To crash upon,
Your shore.

It's the love of fate

When you fall in love.
The muse comes out,
Of the words you speak,
And write upon her pages.
While losing my religion,
Every time,
My pen falls into the spaces,
Where my love rushes in,
To fill in your heart.

A little voice
Speaks from the silence,
When my lips,
I pretend are pressed,
Against the silhouette,
Of your body.
It's the only thing,
That gets me,
Through the darkness,
Of the night without you.
I don't belong here,
Where the only blanket,
Is the cover of shadow.
My body seeks out,
The warmth of your figure,
But nothing compares,
To the feeling of you,
Wrapped up,
Beneath the covers.

Lying in the meadow with you
As April showers,

Drench our bodies with kisses,
From the oceans many miles away,
While tasting your kisses mixed,
With the tears of angels.

There's so much to these things I feel
Where every touch is a reaction,
To a deep emotion I feel for you.
Skin deep emotions,
Down to my soul,
And I feel it in my bones every time.
Every time I touch you,
But my body aches just to feel you,
Touch me, kiss me with the same passion,
The same way you breathe.
The way we make love,
Exposing your embers,
So, I can fan the flames,
Of your desire one more time.
Show me that you thirst for me,
For my everything like I do for you.
That you a driven by your emotions,
Your sensuality and want to express it.
With so much more than words,
But with your fingers, your body.
Show me, I am not alone in wanting,
To build on a memory of your essence,
As our souls write messages along our bodies.

The moon rises in your eyes
When our lips touch,
And I feel weightless.

Just from a kiss,
From a touch,
A feeling,
Of love,
Beneath the stars.

❖ ❖ ❖

If I would have known
All the trouble you caused,
I would've left you alone,
Instead of being caught up,
In the storm of you.
I wish I never meet you,
But that illusion your portrayed,
Was too convening to ignore.
So, I fell for you and all your lies,
At least I can use those red flags to float.

❖ ❖ ❖

Pudding and sweet cakes
That slap together,
Like flap jacks and maple syrup,
But I like my food dipped in honey,
Because there's always room for desert,
When you're on the menu.
A little whip cream topping,
Drizzled with sprinkles,
Cherries and some pineapple slices,
Making you into a sundae,
Slipping and sliding,
Along your frosted curves,
As you squirm from the chill,
Of the ice cream on your delicate form,
Because I'm going to use my tongue,

And share the treat of licking you clean.

Let's play a game
Where I draw your figure,
With a pen.
Tracing over your body,
Making rubbings of each curve,
As I explore,
The twist, turns, bumps and mysteries,
Of your body with ink.
Can I love on you,
With each stroke of my pen,
As it glides along your lips,
Down your neck,
To your breast.
Just tracing the outline,
Of your body,
Because my memory,
Is spotty from the wear of time.
I want to remember your body,
As it speaks to me with sensual desire,
While we make love,
And I take notes to remember your beauty.

Here I am,
Bleeding again,
From a wounded heart,
My red hands,
Stained,
With madness and tears,
From your ivory lies.
What was about him?

That made you want him,
Over someone like me.
All your words,
Can't fix this,
As we fall away,
And out of love.

Wondering
Lost in the rain,
Pouring over the wreckage,
Of my discarded life.
Many times,
I return to the image of you,
And that last kiss,
Where everything unraveled.

Rain-soaked dreams
And melancholy days,
Where we were lost,
In the magic of it all.
Gazing,
Into the wreckage,
Of your soul,
Behind your eyes.
Where I help rebuild you.

Dance with me
One last time,
Before we part,
And we return,

To the silent wanting,
Of each other once more.

Unlock all the secrets
That block you,
It's a simple notion,
One the will rock you.

It's a **matter of tick tock**
When we run around the block,
In a hurry to spend our time,
Just hanging out on the dock.

Being lost in the stars
Instead of bars,
And quick drink saloons,
Just to unlock the meaning of stars.

I was amazed
Being here,
Lying in your arms.
This was a place,
I haven't been,
In a long time.
Your smile was warm,
As you held me tight,
Listening,
To your heartbeat.

It was magic,
Being held like this.
You kiss my forehead,
As you hugged me closer,
Our legs entwined,
Closing my eyes,
Wishing this moment,
Would never end.

Shooting

Reflecting the twilight,
Of dancing dreams,
In your blue eyes.
It's a mesmerizing,
Sight counting stars there.

In a gilded cage

Is where my heart is.
It's a beast,
Riddled with madness,
Behind bone.
I keep it,
Tucked away,
Because,
There's no reason,
To release it.
I haven't,
Been given a reason,
To trust someone,
With the keys to those locks,
So, there it sits in chains.
Either they break it,

I break it,
And it bleeds.
Please, don't feel pity for it,
Or even me.
I know the sadness,
That hope brings,
The moment a key,
Turns the stones,
Within those locks,
And the bonds,
Are broken.
That's Pandora's box,
And I know the pain,
She felt,
Once the chest was opened.

The vibrant beauty of your eyes
Left me spellbound by your vibe.
So, I feel violently in love,
With your ferocity.
And the madness your spell,
Took hold of me,
Left me breathless,
As I found myself,
Losing all reason,
To control my senses,
When you touched me,
Because I felt your magic,
Enter me and took control,
Of all of me.
Just from looking into the eyes,
Of a goddess with blue eyes.

It's a long walk home
When your heart is broken.
Each step you carry the weight,
Of the pieces,
Which burrow into your soul,
And you fight back tears,
Along a dirt road.

Life happened
And a beautiful romance,
Blossomed of a nostalgic bliss,
Between two love struck lovers.
Just you and I,
As we found the beauty of kisses,
Holding hands,
And a bliss of finding comfort,
Of two souls,
Learning to share one dream.

Somewhere
Between daydream specter,
And a lucid sleep.
I found shards of happiness.
Pieces of memories,
I had long forgotten.
Holding them,
In my palms,
As they play,
Like an old movie.
Those times,
Of walking,

Barefoot in the summer sun,
As the leaves danced in the breeze.
The scent of her perfume,
Carrying on the wind,
As you lay drifting off to sleep,
From her gentle touch,
It's feeling at peace,
Being in young love.

◆ ◆ ◆

Summer scene
It's the warmth of your skin,
Being here in the meadow,
Where the wildflowers grow.
Where you wild kisses,
Entangle and entice me,
To drink deeper from your tender lips.

◆ ◆ ◆

My lady love
Holding joy at the edge of sorrow,
The girl who loved the demon,
Hidden within me.
All those trivial things,
The complacent endless fables,
She weaved together,
With every kiss,
Strung together like pearls,
Against the velvet night sky.
For all the things I regret,
Was watching your love,
Slowly dying as the days,
Drifting from one hand to the next.

No matter how much I fought,
To win your faith back,
With my undying love.
Your out reaching arms,
Withered like vines,
And died,
In the summer of my chaos.
I could only watch,
As you walked away,
Dragging pieces of my heart,
Along the jagged floor,
Smearing the inky blood stained,
Pebbles in your wake.

◆ ◆ ◆

She collected broken hearts
Thrown together in a jars
A bubbling soup she flavored,
With her sorrow, tears,
And lingering doubt.
She knew her craft,
With every heart she took,
From the collection of men,
She gathered them all.
Laced together with string,
That hung around her neck.
A broken trophy,
Tied with a knot,
On the end.

◆ ◆ ◆

Jar of hearts
A fist full of clubs,
The Harley Quinn,

Plays with a loaded deck,
When it comes to love,
And twisted madness.

◆ ◆ ◆

I harbor them
Here and there,
Old lies in my vase,
Where I try to erase them.
Little harmless lies,
I spoke to you,
Careless words,
Spoken to you,
As we dance around,
The topic of love.
Your lies were louder,
And blinked us,
From this place of trust,
With every lie you spoke.

◆ ◆ ◆

These fragile **heartstrings of mine**
Create beautiful melodies plucked by a goddess,
Whose silhouette is burned into my mind.
Darkness found me when the light of her love dimmed,
And I became lost in the shadows of madness,
Searching for the flame of a scarlet goddess.
Oh, how I miss the warmth of her frame,
When I curl up beside her,
Feeling her body rise and fall.
I couldn't help testing the fates,
As I placed slow pecks upon your neck,
Tracing your shoulder slightly.
My desire wasn't for sex,

Or the feeling of release,
But of gratitude of being in the arms of a goddess,
And running my fingers through the flames,
Of crimson silk that adorn your head.
Bittersweet memories,
Course through my mind,
Of wanting to feel your love,
And the touch of your fingers,
Like before when it was all new,
And it felt like you cared about me.

It's the quiet embrace
When the light of dusk,
Creeps into our room.
The natural light,
Is intoxicating,
As I lay here,
Watching angel sleep,
Wrapped up in my arms.

You can **embrace your dreams**
One fragment at a time,
As you close your arms around them,
Because dreams gather at the center of your heart.

Solace
A blissful desire,
Of feeling,
I find myself longing for.

With every breath,
Just to breathe you in.
And hearing those words,
Do you promise me,
You will love me forever?
Even if it was for a little while,
Or a lifetime of stardust.

◆ ◆ ◆

White petals fall
Of cherry blossoms.
Like snowflakes in winter.
Collecting in your hair.

◆ ◆ ◆

Those are the memories
Of a kiss beneath the cherry blossoms,
In the springtime.
It was sad,
Watching the cherry blossoms,
Whither and fall,
Like the leaves of autumn.

◆ ◆ ◆

Those aren't freckles
But kisses from melted stardust,
When you flew through the heavens,
On wings of fire.
They're a reflection,
Of all the stars in the universe,
Each one so unique,
Than the first one you discovered.
Flakes of broken worlds

Dirty snowballs,
That were scattered upon the solar winds.
Collected and poured into a fiery beauty,
Who could melt your heart,
With just a kiss from her lips,
And set your mind a blaze.

◆ ◆ ◆

I miss the **taste of spring**
On your lips when we kissed.
It was amazing,
The memory of you.
Like breathing,
After surrendering,
And being released,
From the crush of the waves.
Staring into the amber color,
Of your iris.
And tracing the outline of your face,
Like the ocean washing away the shore.
It was a carnival of madness,
All the chaos of love,
Where I found myself,
Caught up in the storm of you.
Just riding the winds,
Of your smile and kisses,
Because it was the only thing,
I could grasp when you and I collide.

The **first steps** of May
After hiding in the dark of winter,
Waiting on spring.

He was the viper
The lies that hide in the weeds,
He told you with his tongue,
Between your legs.

The house on the lane
Was broken and tattered
A shambled mess,
Where only ghost of memories,
Played within the shadows.
She wanted to explore,
So, she dragged me alone,
And that's how I fell,
Broke my crown,
While falling for the girl,
Who loved shadows,
And playin,
In the ruins of old houses,
Pretending,
We were living the memories,
Inside of those walls.

Do you know **that feeling?**
No matter what you do,
It feels like the world,
Is passing you by?
And no matter how much,
You rush to catch up,
Somehow,

You're still watching it all,
Go by in a swirl, blur, or a flash.

❖ ❖ ❖

You're a prism of beauty
One where I could be lost,
Staring into your eyes.

❖ ❖ ❖

The words are **difficult to connect**
Into something worth talking about.
I'm so tired.
It's that kind of fatigue,
Where you don't want to speak,
Because the worlds,
Are just a jumbled mess.
I've grown weary,
Of speaking words,
And writing them on the page.
Everything just aches,
Like an open wound,
And I find myself bleeding,
From the festering rot of life.
Where happiness,
Is so hard to win.

❖ ❖ ❖

What is it about me
Where I always fail,
At finding love.
Even when I don't search,
It's not my intention,
In trying to find this.

I've let go of things,
And a thousand ghostly faces,
Of women who I have loved,
Perhaps been infatuated with.
One-by-one each was a beauty,
In my mind.
But they didn't want me,
Or even knew I existed.
Yet, there were moments,
Where it seemed,
Like there was a spark.
What did I do,
To make that spark die.
I'm not perfect,
However, it seems I have to be.
I just don't get it.
What is so wrong,
With wanting to fall in love.
Wanting something more,
Then a one-night stand?
I feel so lost and alone.
Why do I attract the wrong people?
Hell, I take a bath, what the actual fuck?

Riding **Jasmine's magic carpet**
I traced the floral designs,
Along the red background of your shirt.
The striking color,
Matched your lips.
Maybe a few shades darker,
For your crimson locks.
I wish I could be there,
Wrapped up in your arms again,
Maybe feel you lying next to me in the dark.

Part of me wants to lay my head,
Upon your chest one last time.
Another wants to suckle at your nipples,
When your shirt has fallen by the wayside.
Replacing the floral designs,
For the silky touch of your skin,
Beneath my fingertips.
As I draw you closer dipping further,
Along your curves of your slender frame.
Kissing your hips.
Taking the plunge,
Into the depths of you,
And marvel at the creation of a woman.
Tasting your pleasure,
And counting the sparks between orgasms,
As your eyes light up.
I would lose myself in the divine beauty of you.
In sharing a connection when I plug into you,
Become one flesh for a time,
Letting chemicals flow beneath the sheets,
Feeling the magic of you,
As I feel you climax,
When we join the cosmic stardust of pleasure.

◆ ◆ ◆

She was **struck by wanderlust**
So moved from place to place,
Searching for her dreams.

◆ ◆ ◆

Those **dreams made of wonder**
Where she roamed,
Wanderlust of beauty,
Of those magic moments.

◆ ◆ ◆

Only she could quench my wanderlust
With the touch of her hands,
And her lips.

◆ ◆ ◆

She rose with **the dawn**
And like the mist,
Hope found her way,
To rise with the sun.
She watched the rays,
Of a new day,
Chase away the night.

◆ ◆ ◆

Close your eyes
She whispered,
As we drew closer,
Like a moth,
I dove into the flames,
To kiss her waiting lips.

◆ ◆ ◆

We moved closer
As we held hands,
Walking down the aisle,
Where two paths,
Become one,
Closing our souls,
In the endless circle,
Of a ring.

◆ ◆ ◆

You're a vision
Of a sweet dream,
Of imperfection,
Of life,
Of creation,
Of beauty.
All of these things,
Lie deep within you.
A sweet figure,
Of divine quality,
Of light,
Which I find myself,
Dumb struck,
And awestruck,
By the light,
That burn within you.

◆ ◆ ◆

Home is **where she was**
Who raced to greet me,
With a fearless embrace.
My fingers and palms,
Strummed along her curves,
As I plucked her heartstrings.
It was a lovely memory,
Every time,
And her heartbeat,
Was the drum,
We danced too,
So many times,
Late at night just swaying,
We did this together.

Long after the music stopped,
Just lost in the moment of us.

As is,
She said.
While looking,
At her reflection.
I wrapped my arms,
Around her waist.
Whispering in her ear,
Be the light,
That light,
You radiate,
Through your eyes.
Not the ones,
The world,
Uses to gaze upon you.
I love you, as is.
As you were then,
As you are now.
The beauty,
Of a woman,
Changing and growing,
Into a magical being.
Those stretch marks,
You wish would go away.
Are love scars,
Because you bared,
A child.
We created life together.
They're the marks of love,
Of hope between two people.
Your curves are yours,
And they speak,

Of soft caresses,
Tender kisses,
Memories of hugs,
And places,
Where we spent nights,
Doing nothing,
But recounting the days,
Stars, planets, and warm summers.
We kept each other warm,
On cold nights,
As I traced the stars,
Along your body.

◆ ◆ ◆

She **rose from the fire**
Like an angel rising from the tomb.
I watched her silhouette,
As the flames licked at her curves,
And bent to her will,
Because her light,
Drove out the darkness at the center of the cosmos.
I watched streams blaze along her body,
Like little rivers of light,
Coursing along the tiny faint hairs,
Along her body.
She was amazing to see,
Every inch of her,
Basking in the rays of sunlight.
Sparks danced in her fiery hair,
Like a waterfall,
Pouring into the stardust lake.
Her naked body,
Was the stars and constellations,
Of the heavens.
It was then I realized,

I had fallen for the goddess of flames,
And I was willing to burn,
Just for a taste of her tender lips,
And discover the secret of the sun's shadow,
In the wake of a fallen star in her arms.

◆ ◆ ◆

I fell in love
With the melody,
Of a brook.
The one where,
You and I,
Passed the time away,
Just listening to nature,
Calling to us from the water.

◆ ◆ ◆

And hope
Is like water,
It's cold, wet,
And quenches,
The deepest hurt,
From a broken heart,
With a single.

◆ ◆ ◆

Why do we hope?
When everything,
Can fall apart in a moment,
Without warning.
I guess,
It's ingrained in us,
To hope and love,

For a better times.

I ignite like a fire balloon
Burning away your joy,
How do you like the flicker,
Of my flame now?
You tossed me aside,
For someone else,
So, now I leave you here,
To burn and rot away,
Into memory for those who care.

I loved **watching her rise**
To meet her storm,
And scatter the clouds.
So, her brilliant light,
Can burn away her sadness,
As she brings herself,
Back to a peace.

Rise above the storm
And scatter the ashes,
Of your foes,
Across the distant shores,
Like a hurricane,
With every inch of your being,
Because you are water made flesh.

She is the only storm
I can bare,
As she rains her sorrows,
Upon my shoulders.
I drown in the sea of her,
And fight to rise,
Against the tide,
Of her sadness.
I feel so lost,
As she beats upon the surface,
Of blue plain of glass,
From the painful memories,
Of her lover's kiss.

It was the **first time**
I had felt anything,
Like this.
Being here,
Wrapped up in your arms.
I felt safe,
And ever since that night,
I can't find my way home.
I'm homesick,
For someone who holds a place,
In another man's arms.
And I don't know what to do?
When you felt like you belonged,
But she's not your woman,
And will never be.

A typewriter with no keys

Is the gag ball to a drunken muse,
Who enjoys late night rants,
While sitting upon your head,
Recounting past loves,
Forgotten adventures,
And painful regrets,
With every turn of a page.
It's a simple madness,
As she whines,
About how you kissed her,
Deep and sensual,
When your pen,
Caressed the pages,
As if was her own body.
Being lost in her eyes,
A thousand times over,
While writing verses,
Upon her body,
Mimicking her curves,
Like the strokes of a brush,
Painting the silhouette of an angel,
Who lost her voice,
Because I hide the keys,
Beneath the pillow where she sits.

Same old feelings
Same old morning,
Where you piece yourself,
Together to face another day.
One... more.... day.
As you cross the room,
To click on the light,
And face down the demon,
Of your addiction,

After splashing water on your face,
Another drop of water,
Drips from your face,
As you trace the alcohol lines,
Of black splotches dotted,
Beneath your eyes, neck, and cheeks.
Was it worth it?
Waking up beside yourself,
And puddle of puke-stained sheets.
It's a memory,
That's all my fingers,
Could grasp,
Of the reality,
When I had,
To call upon myself,
To mend my broken heart,
Because I was the one,
Who could only save me.
It wasn't her,
Or the meaning for her,
To surrender to me,
As her knight in shining armor.
But me,
Only I kept missing the chances,
To rescue myself,
In turning away from the destruction,
Of my wayward heart.

I learned the **secret of love**
By reading the goosebumps,
Written upon your skin.
Its ancient words,
Buried deep within us all,
Where our souls,

Find their connection,
And love deeper.
Those bumps,
Are a language,
Of mystery,
My soul has longed,
To read them,
When we kiss deeply.

◆ ◆ ◆

Goosebumps
Those lumps,
Humps,
Buried beneath your flesh.
The ones,
I bring to the surface,
When I kiss the corners,
Of your soul.
Finding the beauty of you,
Trapped,
And longing to be released,
By my gentle lips,
As you bask in my kisses,
Trailing along your skin.

◆ ◆ ◆

I lie awake
Gazing at the skyline of stars.
Lost in my sense of wonder,
At the night sky,
Trying to figure out,
Which part of heaven,
Is yours.

Across time zones
Is like crossing,
The River Styx,
In search of my eternity,
So, I'll pay the boatman,
Just to hold you again.

Do you know
The meaning of eternity?
It's knowing the tick tock,
Of an imaginary clock,
As the minutes tick by,
Without you.

It was a **couple of days**
After we buried you.
The feelings were still raw,
Now, I was the one,
The world,
Came crashing down upon.
Unsteady shoulders,
Baring the weight,
Of being a brother, father, and mother,
To a young woman,
With the mind of a child.
But you would be proud of her,
And how she has grown,
To be so much more.
All I asked that day,

When I had to find my way,
Mom, you said in your own way,
To be a simple man when that song,
Played on the radio that day.
Those words still remain,
With me as I struggle,
To find my way in life.

◆ ◆ ◆

She walked **among the shadows**
Her silhouette hidden by shade,
Until my touch,
Found the hourglass of her.
Fumbling around in the darkness,
Where the only light I could see,
Was emitted by the beat of your heart.
It was sweet intoxication,
Feeling you in my arms,
While I kissed away the chilly air,
From the curves of your skin.
The night camouflaged,
Your beauty as we made love,
Using our sense of taste and touch,
To guide us in the dark.

◆ ◆ ◆

The waves
Of dreams,
Where the tides,
Of wonder,
Drift over me.
Dreams,
Last for hours,
Gone in a flash.

But what are dreams?
Hopes and wishes,
My heart makes,
Or pieces of memories.
Pieces of a time,
In another world,
One,
Where the life,
You wanted is right there,
Firmly within your grasp.

◆ ◆ ◆

Someday somehow
I'll be able to hold you,
And know what it will be like,
To feel you close to me.

◆ ◆ ◆

It was a dream
One where you and I,
We're holding each other.
It was someplace,
A memory,
Where I was once a child.
Maybe this was the place,
Being with you represented home,
In every form I could imagine.
Holding my scarlet goddess,
Tightly in my arms,
As we snuggled, closer.
A breeze made the leaves,
Dance in the springtime air.
Light shown through,
The transparent green leaves,

Streaks of heaven,
Of something lost to time,
Of a home I once knew,
And found in your arms.
I was safe there,
And the screaming of my insanity,
Died away in the comfort of your arms.
Home,
A memory I long for,
Maybe not in your arms anymore,
But with someone,
I can call home,
Whenever I am near her.

I've never **seen magic**
Like the velvet circle,
Of your iris,
Reflecting shooting stars,
And galaxies,
In starlight of the night sky,
When you blink away,
The tears of stardust.

Did you know
The meaning of love,
Is magic?
It's the creation,
Of something,
By the means,
Of manifesting the will,
To embrace hope,
When two people,

Fall into magic.

Starlight dripped from your tears
When he hurt you.
I was the only one there to wipe away,
Those tears you shed for him,
With scraps of velvet,
Torn from the ribbons left of me.
I was wasted magic,
You wished upon falling stars for.
But my light wasn't bright enough,
To shine where you could see me.
So, I faded from your memory,
And your life as you danced,
Around his flames.
Ignoring your burns,
When you stepped into the fire.
And while he blazed,
Eating away at your embers.
The inferno of him,
Was seeking other women,
While wicking away your essence,
With every touch of his lies.
Now, you lay covered in ashes,
And broken hearted.

◆ ◆ ◆

You think it's hot
Fucking with them.
Mysterious men,
Who hide behind a veil,
Of secrecy.
Those moment of rapture,

As he pushes all your buttons,
Leave you gluttons,
Filled with desire,
For an illusion,
That he holds over you,
Until he pulls away,
The very floor you stand on.

◆ ◆ ◆

She shuttered
As I entered her,
From behind,
I told her,
Don't jump off the bed,
When I started,
To put all my weight,
Upon her hips,
Burying myself,
Deeper into her space.
I felt possessed,
As she pushed back,
With her hips,
Grinding away,
Wanting my seed.
I covered her,
Like a blanket,
As I drove harder,
Into the silk of her,
Silent moans,
Carried in the dim lit room,
As I felt the curve of her back,
Rise to meet my chest.
Kissing away at her neck,
Our fingers intertwined,
And laced together,

I could feel her orgasm,
Rising within her,
So, I steadied my pace,
Because I wanted,
To peak with her.

◆ ◆ ◆

I searched **for your light**
Lost and alone in the darkness,
Searching for a soul's hue,
In the emptiness of the night.
Then I saw a faint glow,
Somewhere,
Between the shadows,
And the ruins of love.
It was there,
Where my search ended.
As I was drawn,
To the magic of your light,
Dancing in the black.

◆ ◆ ◆

Have you ever wondered
If fireflies,
Were once shooting stars?
The way they dance,
In the darkness of the meadows,
Akin to the black of the night sky.

◆ ◆ ◆

Dreaming away
The time goes by,
Wishing you were,

Here in my grasp.
Dreams of whispers,
Drift through my palms,
Where the memories,
Of things,
Dissolve into a mist,
And withers away,
Into the darkness.

◆ ◆ ◆

Dreaming
Dreams,
Dream away,
In wishing things,
Would come true.
Wishing,
Wanting,
To taste your lips,
And dance with you,
For a while.
Fantasies,
A jumbled reality,
Of lost hopes.

◆ ◆ ◆

She was a **singularity**
Something of rare gem,
Among all the mysteries,
Of the world she built.

◆ ◆ ◆

Black rose petals
Made of velvet tears,

Cascade like a waterfall,
Drifting through the garden,
It was her dream,
To be wed,
In a garden of black roses.

The little **yellow car**
Had seen better days,
Of travelling rolling hills,
Through bustling cities,
On a journey of a lifetime.
Until it came to rest,
Here in the meadow,
Overgrown by daisies,
Wildflowers and tall grass,
Rusting away,
But I swear,
If you look at it now,
How the earth,
Has swallowed pieces of it,
And flowers,
Have replaced broken glass,
And weathered parts,
With life.
The little car,
Wears a smile on its bumper.

I've written a hundred unsent texts
Only to delete ever word,
A thousand times more.
Searching for the right words,
To say to a goddess like you,

The right words,
To elicited a response,
Rather than silence.
I play the conversation,
Over and over in my head,
As the words seem to flow,
Only to fade once my fingers,
Start pushing the letters.
It's like there's a broken connection,
Between my fingers, head, and heart.
Because I want to be the man,
You need me to be,
But I can't find the courage,
To bring about simplest change,
In making you mine,
To know the truth,
You had me spell bound at hello.
It was your eyes,
Those dark swirls of heaven,
Laced with sparkling diamonds,
Scattered across a plain of black,
That held me captivated,
And I found myself wanting,
To drown in the waves of your hair,
As those same locks,
Washed over me when I gazed,
Into the vastness of your soul,
The center of the galaxy,
Buried deep inside you.
But these are only words,
Words,
That I'll ease again,
And start over,
Before I find the courage,
To send you another unsent text.

I don't know
Where to begin,
Letting go.
The last time I held you,
All those feelings,
Seemed to disappear.
And all that remained,
Was the feeling of loneliness,
Along with heartache.
What happened to us?
Or was there even a thing?
I felt something,
Then it wasted away into shadows.
I guess it is time to move on,
Even if I offer everything I am,
It would never be enough for you.
Nor would you understand the sacrifice,
I made for you.
I'm not falling upon my sword for you,
Those days are done,
Just like you are.
I'm snuffing out the flame,
To the candle I burned for you,
And throwing it away.
I'm letting go of you.
So someday,
I can find peace within myself,
To bring the things I truly desire,
Into my waiting arms.

I stared **into the dawn**

Of the sun rise,
In the infinity of your iris.
Where I lay,
Upon the shores,
Kissed by an ocean of blue.
And there,
I found peace,
Wrapped up in your arms,
As the tides of your love,
Washed over me.

What words
Would it have took,
For you to remain here.
All those unspoken words,
I wish I had said to you,
Even if it wasn't my place,
To say I love you.

The flames **rose higher**
In the home we built together,
With a touch of her hand,
More things began to burn,
No matter how hard,
I fought to control the flames.

She ran her fingers
Through the tainted water,
Shifting the sands,
And pebbles beneath the surface.

With a wave of her hand,
The water began to clear,
As the ripples,
Reached the edges of the shoreline.

◆ ◆ ◆

How do you **describe home?**
When you find it,
In the arms of a woman.
Only lose it,
And since then,
Every place I have looked,
I can't find my way home.

◆ ◆ ◆

Words carry **a different meaning**
When they're unspoken,
To the ones,
Who are no longer living to hear them.
It was lust
With a little bit of gluttony thrown in,
The way I devoured your body with my eyes and lips.
I traced tender kisses along your neck to your shoulders,
I took pride in my work,
As goosebumps rose beneath your skin.
Greed swept over me in wanting more of you,
Letting my hands slide in places,
Taking you to the point of ecstasy with every kiss.
But I was slow as a sloth,
Making ever touch count,
Every ounce of me.
You tasted my wrath as you felt me enter you,
The way you moaned made the woman,
Passing in the hall envy you.

❖ ❖ ❖

I guess I'm just a memory,
One destined to fade among the pages,
Ink stains and dreams,
Of the man who wasn't there.
Sometimes I wonder if I exist,
Whether people see me,
Or just long enough for a quick joke.

❖ ❖ ❖

I wore the ocean on my shoulders,
While floating in a sea of blue,
Wading in the shallows,
With you by my side,
And the tide washing over me.
Feeling the grit of sand,
Filling my pockets,
And places untouched by sunlight.

❖ ❖ ❖

All the women
Who've graced my life,
One way or another,
You are the most complex.
My head keeps telling me,
I should avoid you,
And never speak to you.
But my heart rebels against me,
No matter how much I fight it,
My heart breaks it chains,
And goes running back to you.

My eyes see the devil,
Hidden beneath your smile.
My mind knows your lies,
And interrupts the silence,
When you don't respond,
As the trust you don't care.
Only my heart clings to you,
Wishing you,
Would show a glimmer of hope,
You really care.
So, every night,
I drag my heart,
Kicking and screaming,
Back to its place,
And slowly rock it to sleep,
Wishing there was a way to break,
The spell you have over it.

It's to the point of frustration,
To carry on a conversation,
When you're the only person speaking,
Because the other person,
Ghosted you long ago.
I get the fatigue of it all,
Trying to find a connection,
Behind a blinking screen,
And string of words.
We are all done with this virus,
Done with the lack of connection,
Lack of touch,
And meaningful memories.
I'm still human you know,
Or does that really matter to you?
If you're not interested,

Then why speak to me?
What did you gain,
From a moment of connection?
Or are you not woman enough,
To actually put yourself out there.
Yeah, yeah.
I've been hurt,
You've been hurt,
I'm just as protective of myself,
As you are of yourself.
You have no right,
To touch my soul,
And walkaway.

◆ ◆ ◆

I thirst for you as I dream,
Not in a lustful way,
But in the way a lovers desire,
Aches for the feeling,
Of you next to me.
The feeling of loving a woman,
Who I've longed to touch,
Through the atoms of space.
A faceless woman,
Who I hope would love me,
With the same ferocity,
I would give to her.
Dreaming of her,
And her silhouette,
Dancing in the starlight,
With someone instead,
Of empty shadows.
Would she want to know,
The meaning of passion?
As we burn in the dark night,

Letting our light embrace us.
I just want one moment,
With her,
Even if it lasts for a second,
Or a lifetime,
Just to kiss her lips,
And taste the effervescent stardust,
Lingering from collapsed stars,
That created the beauty,
Who graces my dreams.

❖ ❖ ❖

All is well
When you don't feel.
I really don't like feelings,
They muck things up.
When,
You have to search for them,
And then try to understand them,
Like they're some kind of child.

❖ ❖ ❖

What is it like
Making love to an angel?
Is it liking the cold rain,
On a hot summer's day?
As the scent of rain,
Overwhelms your senses.
Feeling the cool sensation,
Of raindrops kissing your skin.
Or it's the opposite,
And kissing her,
Is like making love to fire.
The flames lick away your fears,

And the ashes and embers,
Of her body,
Warm you beneath the covers.
Laying in a crumbled mess,
Legs entwined melted as one.
Perhaps making love to an angel,
Is so pure,
That it involves all the elements,
Just to feel the stardust,
Coursing through her veins,
When you touch her skin.

◆ ◆ ◆

I long for things,
That are a dream for me,
In wanting to be desired.
That there is someone,
Who generally,
Wants to be with me,
At end of the day.
Wants to hold me,
Run their fingers,
Through my hair,
And my beard.
Lace me with kisses,
And hugs,
Because these are things,
I would do for her.
Lying in the bed,
Or the couch,
Watching movies,
Or listening to the rain,
Watching shooting stars,
While being hugged,
And feeling loved,

Beyond all measure,
Which seems like,
I have better luck,
At finding Bigfoot,
Or Jim Hoffa,
Before finding a woman,
Who would do this,
And so many other things.

◆ ◆ ◆

I've fallen for the dark of you,
The faded light that shines,
It flickers and dances,
Like a dying flame.
I've seen your edges,
Jagged and straight,
And cut myself on the flanges.

◆ ◆ ◆

It's your touch
That sends me,
Into a frenzy.
Gentle,
As you trace,
My frame,
Every moment,
I play in my head,
As the memory,
Plays,
Like a movie.
Your fingers were soft,
As they found,
The places,
That you longed for,

I longed for.
One more kiss,
From your lips to mine,
As we searched,
For a reason,
To remain here.
Staring into your eyes,
Those beautiful pearls,
Of mystery,
And desire.
It was all or nothing,
She said after kissing me,
From small pecks,
To long deep kisses,
Until she rested her lips,
Upon my own,
As we drank,
From our thirsty desire,
Of a fantasy.

I want to **burn with you**
And feel the flames,
Burn away our edges,
Melding us together.
Being set ablaze,
By your smile,
As we touch.

How calm **is the storm**
In your eyes,
Beneath the ocean of your iris.

Because your eyes
Tell a story,
Of being brave,
In your darkest moments.

Etching
Those eyes,
Where I got lost,
So many times,
When we meet.
She was burned into my mind,
Etched into my soul,
With every kiss that graced my lips.
And I was drowning in those flames,
Setting my passion ablaze,
Every time I touch you.
Unquenched emotions,
Seemed to race through my veins,
With a touch of your hands,
I felt your heat,
As you lingered,
Tracing your fingers,
Along my edges,
Setting them on fire,
As you welded your body,
To mine.
Letting our chemicals mingle,
Stoking the embers,
As we built our romance,
From the sparks of a glance.

A mosaic of memories,
Run through my mind,
Of how we used to kiss.
It was like that,
As I sit here,
Watching you kissing,
Someone else for forever.

Mosaic of dreams
Fade,
Drift away,
And die.
Like the feeling,
Of your touch,
Upon my skin.
It's just an echo,
Of things,
As they should've been,
Only a specter.
Dwells beneath my skin,
Reenacting those feelings,
Of my desire for you.

♦ ♦ ♦

Fighting
And losing ground,
Because your toxic grasp,
Has me fixed tight,
And I'm lost in you.
No matter,

How I struggle,
To overcome,
Those lips,
And thighs,
Drag me further down,
A long rabbit hole of darkness.
Every step I take,
I find myself slipping,
And stumbling back to your arms.
The madness of your sex,
And the venom of your kiss,
Poisons my mind,
Where I am transfixed,
On your every word,
Like some wayward religion,
I have to bare my soul,
Just to survive,
Being nailed to your cross.

Toxic dreams
And memories,
Of black lies.
Ones that torment,
My hopes of freedom.
It's a liquid solution,
With a soul purpose,
To drown my sorrows,
And it comes in many flavors,
It's the only thing,
That dries you out,
With every drop,
That alters your mind,
And flushes life from your bones.

◆ ◆ ◆

A frozen tear
Is all that remains,
Of my love for you.
Wrapped neatly,
In a handkerchief,
Stuffed in a box,
High upon the shelf,
With all the other tears.
It's a wound that won't heal,
One that I've ripped apart,
Every time,
I see your face,
Or hear you call my name.
Then I look into your eyes,
And all of those times,
You broke my heart,
Have me forgetting,
The pain of it all.
The fear of loving you,
Should cancel out,
These buried feelings,
That rise like a dead thing,
Seeking to make a meal,
Out of what remain of me.

◆ ◆ ◆

The **beauty of a rose**
And her thorns,
Are graceful,
When she allows you,
Into her garden of mystery.
Her skin is delicate,

Like her petals,
Which adorns her curves.
She is magic,
Wonder and love.
Because that,
Is the definition of a rose.
She is the fragrance,
Of bittersweet memories,
When I prick myself,
Upon her thorns,
As I try to embrace,
The woman lying beneath,
All those scars.
But she is a rose,
And blossoms,
In places where light,
Barely shines.
And....I...fell,
Upon her thorns,
Letting my blood,
Mingle among her petals,
Staining them red,
And with every ounce,
Of my strength,
To love the woman,
Beneath her cage of thorns.

Your words
Tore away,
Pieces of my skin,
Laying me bare.
Every sentence,
Spelled death,
Of our make-believe world.

I tried to cover myself,
With the pages,
Of the book,
You beat me with,
Adding fuel to the fire
Burning me alive,
Deep within myself.
As I wage a war inside and out,
I have no refuge,
From the demons,
Who wait in the shadows,
And darkest corners of my skull.
Places you once touched,
With that brilliant light of yours,
Before something tripped,
And I became the focus of your rage,
Tearing away all that made me human,
Until a thin sheet of paper,
Remained of the man I once was.

You pulled at my flesh,
Tearing away those arrows,
And slings of madness,
I sustained on the battlefield.
Laying me down,
You gave me water,
And cleaned my wounds,
Tending to the things,
That made you an angel of mercy,
Silent, beautiful, and breathtaking.
I felt the warmth of your touch,
And it coursed through my veins.
You weep,
Was the only thing,

I noticed.
Icy tears fell from blue eyes,
And it was the last thing,
I remembered feeling,
As you closed your hand,
Clutching my soul,
Within your grasp,
To carry me,
Across the rainbow bridge,
With all the other warriors.

Those twisted words
Teased by the shapely red,
Of your tenders lips.
The ones that tasted bitter,
From a lie on her lips.
And the echoes,
Of fibs you told,
Just to tie me up in knots,
Where you left me no choice,
Because I can't undo,
All the wrongs,
You said I've done.

Your kiss
Is intoxicating,
And I am so drunk,
On your effervescent lips,
That my fingers,
Stumble all over your body,
Searching for a place to hold onto,
As I grasp for the slippery slopes,

Of those curves.
As you get lost in me,
In trying to rip my clothes,
Away from my body,
From the intoxicating lust,
Of looking into my eyes.

◆ ◆ ◆

This is why we've got to touch,
Sometimes words are not enough,
When your intoxicated by the spell,
Of the first kiss romance,
And the realization that love exists.

◆ ◆ ◆

Dip me into **the color of you**,
And let me paint your beauty,
On the canvas of you.
Let me love you,
With every stroke of my brush,
Touch your curves,
As I draw circles,
Lines and dreams,
From the fantasy of your kiss.
My imagination,
And your body,
Is my heaven,
When I draw you close,
As your heartbeat,
Guides my brush,
In making,
A portrait for a goddess.

Borders and edges
Metaphors and similes,
Of love and hate,
The bitter truth of lies,
We tell ourselves,
When we fall out of love.
Out of laughter,
And hope,
Where dreams die,
Because the things,
We held onto,
For so long,
Was the hope,
Of being loved,
Deeply,
Without hesitation.

◆ ◆ ◆

The **elegance of long shadows**
As the sun rises and sets,
Along the walls,
Through the bed they run,
It's the only thing stirring in this room.
As I lay in my bed,
Watching the day slip away,
Slip away,
Like a breath during a sigh.
Depression takes away your ambition,
And lies to you in the silence of your mind.
Not about unworthiness at times,
Or are you good enough.
But the desire of wanting to accomplish more,
Than turning over to reach for the covers,
To draw against the chill of your frame,

Or shutout the sunlight that invaded your dreams.
Dreams where you were free,
And not struggling to stagger to your feet,
To relieve yourself of last night's drinks,
Only stopping to look at the face in the mirror,
Before turning out the light to stroll the hall,
To a cold lonely bed.

◆ ◆ ◆

Memories
Those **atoms of dreams**,
Laced together,
By the hope of things,
You once kissed,
And tasted forever.
It's a light show of brilliance,
Being in your headspace,
Where memories are created,
In a heartbeat of a moment.

◆ ◆ ◆

There's no words to express,
The pain I feel,
Because there is no one,
Who wants to know me.
People wade in the shallows,
Of other people's lives,
And can't swim in the depths,
Of true friendship or love.
They are afraid to swim,
In a sea of me or you.
So, they only get their feet wet,
Standing on the shoreline,
But when the tides,

Rise to their knees,
They retreat to high ground,
Letting others,
Drift and die alone.

Winding roads
Of rising asphalt,
To meet the tires,
As they roll along.
The scenery changes,
With ever new mile,
On this wanderlust journey,
Of a life filled with hope.

I whisper into your ear,
And trace the tiny roads,
Of lines along your face,
To your gleaming smile,
And taste your tender lips,
Before I drift off to sleep.

The memories
Crush me and turn me,
Inside out from within.
They play over in my head,
As connect the dots,
To all the things,
That made us undone.

First day of school,
And the story began,
Of a secret crush,
And the memories,
Of her silhouette,
Where her sweater,
Hung around her shoulders,
Draped by her red hair.
She brought about change,
In the being within me,
She was like a breath,
I drew with every gasp,
I made.
As I longed,
To taste her lips,
Like she,
Was the only drink,
My body craved,
To quench my thirst.

❖ ❖ ❖

It was magical
Those moments,
That I wish,
I could relive,
Over again,
Slowly.
Hungry,
To feel you,
Cling to me,
In the embrace,
Of what lovers do,
Being so close you,
That when she moves,

You feel it,
Beneath your skin,
When you kiss.

◆ ◆ ◆

The remorse of vanity
A dying shadow,
Of sand slipping,
Through the hourglass,
One grain at a time,
As she wastes away,
Searching for mister right.
A knight to slay her demons,
And take her away,
On a long journey,
A way from the madness,
Of her everyday life.
So, she waits,
Changing colors,
Of her makeup,
Like a chameleon,
Searching,
For a combination,
To unlock the mystery of him.
If she only knew,
That she was strong,
Stronger than the men,
Who used her up,
And discarded her.
That she was the one,
Who could rescue her,
From all the sadness,
That broke her heart,
Into so many pieces.
But those dreams,

Never happened,
As she continues,
The never-ending story,
Of being a pawn,
In someone else's game.

◆ ◆ ◆

What have I done?
My heart says,
Over and over again,
When it speaks.
It carries on conversations,
To those who would listen,
Through my words,
Stained upon the pages,
Of notebooks and digital print.
The blood it bleeds,
Isn't red,
But black and white,
And the ink runs,
When my broken heart,
Draws lines with smeared tears.
Tears I shed for her,
Someone,
I knew,
Only to watch,
Her fade away into oblivion,
Like so many other faces,
Of lost lovers and friends.
A broken mess,
Of scattered pieces,
Left to glimmer in the darkness,
Like a thousand stars,
Which my heart reflects upon.
It says why me?

In trying to understand,
Where things went wrong,
Pouring over the memories,
Of things that were lost,
Before,
They had the chance to grow.
It was like for a brief moment,
The light shined in the darkness,
On a single rose to bloom,
And die,
While being crushed by a landslide.
Wiping out beauty,
In a cold world.

Reflections of a time
Locked away in a moment,
Between you and I.
Everything stands,
Perfectly still.
Only you and I play here,
Where we push the boundaries,
Of our love and imagination.
Here we feel,
The shockwaves,
Of our touch,
As it resonates,
Through our beating hearts.
Every breath,
Every thought,
Lasts forever,
In this moment,
Alone with you.

You can't change the past,
No matter how much bleach you use.
Wiping away a clean slate,
Doesn't wash away the memories,
Of you touch,
Let alone your tender kisses,
Or the nights of your warm body,
Strung close to mine,
In my embrace.

❖ ❖ ❖

Tossed about
On the stormy seas,
Of a turbulent love.
Riding out the storm,
Was easy,
But you made waves,
For me to climb,
So, I drowned in your fury.

❖ ❖ ❖

The **memory of your smile**
Seems so far away to me.
Even though those moments,
Were only yesterday,
In my mind's eye.
Alas,
It all fades away,
In the end.

❖ ❖ ❖

Tear away the scars

And beneath,
You will find a broken child.
Sadness comes in waves,
As madness breaks down,
Every fiber of my being.
A child learns the meaning of loss,
Six months into his life,
An unwanted child by his father,
A mother stood her ground,
To her son from being casted into the flames,
Of the fireplace,
Over the years,
Molested by a close friend,
Brought about a parent's rage,
And the isolation,
Of becoming a sheltered child.
Years of therapy,
And a wrapped sense of reality,
Where his imagination was his only escape,
From the world around him.
Dropping out of school,
And out of life,
Before finding the courage,
To become a man,
But a failure at love.

I caught an eclipse
Just a slight glimpse,
Of an angel.
And her light,
Was so bright,
I could barely,
See her silhouette,
Bathed in light.

All the darkness,
Buried deep inside of me,
Was burned away,
By her glow.
And like a moth,
To a flame,
I wanted,
To grasp,
Those burning embers,
Of a dancing fire,
With my bare hands.
But my scars ached,
As the flames rose higher,
Standing next to her,
I had to run away,
For the fear,
Of being burned again.

Don't you wish
That you could find,
Someone who wants,
To take that leap with you.
No halfway,
Because their love is endless,
For your heart,
And they're all in.

Endless dreams
Followed by nightmares.
A day that changed your life,
After watching the crescendo,
Of your mom's final hours alive,

And the beginning of new life,
Without her.

◆ ◆ ◆

Solivagant journey
Where I thought,
By now my path,
Wouldn't be lonely.
Yet time is cruel,
On this winding road,
Of dusty trails,
And endless miles.
Sometimes I wonder,
If I'll ever find a woman,
To call my home,
While resting in her arms.
Still the road twists and turns,
And every smiling face,
Becomes a memory,
Where I wish she laid naked,
Next to me.
All the things,
I gave up,
Chasing after dreams,
Only to watch them slip,
From my fingertips,
Like watching you,
Walking out my life,
And into the arms,
Of another man.

◆ ◆ ◆

It all unravels
Like a rope,

One strain,
At time.
Was the tension,
That caused the rift,
As the things,
Came undone,
Beneath the bridge,
We strung together,
With each kiss,
And folded hands,
Building rungs,
Along our path.
One bitter word,
And the bridge snapped,
Unwinding everything,
In the blink of an eye.
And all I could do,
Was grasp for the fraying ends,
Of a dying love.

It's roulette
As the numbers flash,
Waiting the ball to land.
Or maybe it's with sex,
Pointed at my head,
Waiting for her to pull the trigger,
So, I can find a release,
From a bullet to my head,
Or the TNT,
Of built-up emotions,
Like an atom bomb,
Inside my head,
Being deemed a man,
But some women,

Want to tear away the title.
So here I am nowhere to go,
Nowhere to turn,
To vent all this crazy,
Wrapped up inside this frame,
And the moment,
I let go of my demons,
You label me a Beta Male.
Stripping away my dignity,
As a man.
This is what you wanted,
In a man being the dominate one,
Until he's at his breaking point,
Then you spin chamber,
Making yourself the battered one,
When I express myself,
And free my demons,
Because you take away,
My only means of finding peace,
In speaking my troubled heart.

Paper
My only friend,
The one,
I tell my secrets too.
It's the only thing,
That knows my dreams,
All my lies,
My fantasies,
And desires.
The things,
That weigh me down.

It may tear,
Become stained,
From time,
But it hides all my pain,
In the words of ink,
I write when I am alone.

♦ ♦ ♦

Falling **down the rabbit hole**
Tumbling, fumbling,
With me lagging behind,
As my wayward heart,
Slides into the abyss.
If you never spoke to me,
Or me seeing,
How deep blue your iris was,
I would've been fine,
Now I'm lost in the what if,
The what if you're the one,
The one who holds the keys,
To my gilded heart's cage,
And I have longed to feel your touch.

Do you know what a mystery is?
It's wondering,
When I look into your eyes,
If the light that shines in you,
Flickers for me.

Loneliness is a mystery
One minute you're fine,
In your solitude.
Then you see someone,
And ache,
From the sting of your freedom.
You wonder would this person,
Want to be a part of your life,
And break the silence,
With the sound of their existence.

◆ ◆ ◆

Write your pain on my heart.
Let pen be your sounding board,
And ink be the end of your pain.
Let this comfort make legible love,
Scribbled on my soul, for.
If my admiration be loose leaf sheets,
Notate the way you blow me away.

◆ ◆ ◆

Collaboration between Cat Francis and Nitejokertn.

What if I told my story different?
Maybe I'm a king,
Instead of a pauper this time.
Maybe I'm the guy strong enough to lead,
Perhaps I am the one who changed my stars,
Where they align to be with you, for me, everything.
What would I have missed out on?
Less pain?
Few memories,
Who knows.
But what if?

What if I could change the world,
Change others,
Where they found inspiration,
In the words I share?

Dating isn't the problem
It's trying to summon your courage,
After many failed attempts,
To build a friendship,
That leads to something more,
Than fighting your way out of the friend zone.
Not to mention dealing with specters,
Ghost and scammers.
Because you can't take people seriously,
Or they weave way too many lies,
To know where the truth begins.
You're ready to accept the failure of things,
Before the first words leave their mouth.
It makes you want to give up,
And watch the opportunity of a lifetime,
Simple walk out the door.
Then again you get played,
Like an old song that echoes,
Off the corners of your mind for years.

◆ ◆ ◆

Did he hear you calling to him?
Deep within the marble,
Where the artist broke you free,
From your rocky prison?
Just so I can marvel at your beauty,

A crafted silhouette of a woman.

What does it take
To speak the words,
That release you,
Set you free,
To manifest a dream,
Of someone I have longed,
To hold in my arms.
Does it take,
Calling back all,
That was lost to me,
All the energy,
I placed into people,
Places or things?
All the tears,
I've shed,
All this pain,
I've endured,
Of longing,
Only to have things,
To play out like they have.
Sitting here,
Alone in my castle,
High upon the hill.
It's the bottom,
Of a lonely spiral,
Trying to find the strength,
To carry on.

I consume you
With every breath I take,

Clinging to your every word,
As I get my fix,
Gazing into the blue,
LSD of your iris.
With every kiss,
Your drug dances in my veins,
Making me lose control,
As I fall deeper into you.
The hallucinations of your body,
Of sweet sex,
Have me struggling,
To grasp my reality,
As we make love.
Hearts race,
From the marathon,
Of chemicals,
Coursing through our bodies,
As we crash upon each other,
coming down from our high.

Here we are
Alone,
With only the sound,
Of the roaring waves,
Being drowned out,
By the beating of our hearts.
And in this moment,
It's like time stood still,
As I swam in the ocean,
Of your green eyes.
Tasting the sea,
Mingled as it traced your lips.

Waves trashed us,
Washing away the sand,
That gathered beneath us.
Cold from the air,
Warm from the sea,
As it cradled us,
In the fading light of the day.

❖ ❖ ❖

It's like watching
The sunsetting,
Being on the edge of despair.
Wanting to hold onto a memory,
As it slips thru your fingers,
And slowly fades,
As you claw away at the ribbons,
Streaming into the emptiness of consciousness.

❖ ❖ ❖

The **tragedy of knowing**
What life is like without you.
Drowning in a lover's tragedy,
As the clock ticks time away.
I thought you were the one,
And it all just fell away,
No matter how much I tried.

❖ ❖ ❖

If love was an object,
It would have scratches,
From where I grasped onto it,
With all my might,

Alas,
The fragile glass,
Slipped from my hands,
From being drenched in my tears,
And shattered,
When you walked away.

◆ ◆ ◆

The darkest desires of my heart,
Can't be expressed with words,
Because you have written them off,
With a wave of a hand.
Those secret desires you keep hidden.

◆ ◆ ◆

Wasted dreams
Lie scattered,
Among the derelicts,
Of other forgotten plans.
Forgotten memories,
Junk and trash,
You've discarded,
When the gales of love,
Blistered and torn,
Wore away at us.
I'll admit,
I was under your spell,
But I thought we shared,
Something more,
Than a simple kiss.

Forgotten,

But **not forgiven**,
Was my thoughts,
Once my feelings,
When we fell apart.
I can't,
Hold onto the bitterness,
Of a dying love.
So, I've set it free,
To wonder with you,
Because I'm not,
Going to bound myself,
To hating someone,
Who couldn't feel.

Already gone
Before the minutes,
Poured away in the hourglass.
Before your scent faded,
From my skin,
After we made love.
Only the sound,
Of a closing door,
Echoing through the silence.

Collecting rust
As time moves on,
When the things,
We once treasured,
Became forgotten things.
Instruments of design,
Collecting dust,
In the corner of our minds.

Where we once played,
In the memories of youth,
Laughing,
Singing away the memories,
Of times we knew we were giants.

◆ ◆ ◆

Impossible
These hopes,
Dreams,
Feelings.
Sometimes,
I feel,
Like I'm out of place,
That I don't belong here,
Being the man,
I am.
Wanting something,
It seems,
Is so unheard of,
These days.
Where the thought,
Of love,
Scares people.
Feelings,
Don't reach below,
The surface of things.
Because people fear,
Drowning,
In knowing

◆ ◆ ◆

Is love possible?
Even if I left the door open,

Would you swim,
Into the deep with me?
Where we can drown,
In the depths of our love?
So many times,
I was the only one,
Leaping to my death,
While they watched me fall.
Are you brave enough,
To take that step with me,
In learning how to love,
Unconditionally,
Without reservations?
Truly.
Are you strong enough,
To let me be your man.

Love was impossible
Where fear of being hurt,
Was the only familiar,
I have come to understand.
Running back,
To the pain of memories,
A familiar comfort,
Where loneliness,
Is my shield,
And the only shelter,
To guard me,
Against the unknown,
Of being in love,
Because what I thought was love,
Was a one-sided affair,
Where I lost everything,
Even though I gained myself,

The fear of desire,
Of being met,
On the field of love,
And finding someone,
Who equals the love,
I express unconditionally.

◆ ◆ ◆

Unending
Is the feeling,
I get,
When my fingers,
Are laced between yours,
Here beneath the harvest moon,
We dance,
In-between the shadows.
As the song plays,
Weaving through moonbeams,
As our silhouettes mingles,
Among the fallen leaves.
The night air is chilly,
As we drawing in closer,
Letting our bodies,
Warm us from our embrace.
I kissed your lips,
And in a moment,
Everything,
Fell away,
As time stood still.

◆ ◆ ◆

It's the only thing
That holds you up,
With every word,

As the lyrics,
Become,
Your personal anthem.
The melody of music,
It's only fitting,
That the word Mus,
Is at the beginning,
Because,
It is the first piece,
To the puzzle of you,
In building the broken you,
As the music,
Lifts you,
From your darkness moments,
And sets you,
Back on solid ground.

He had a taste of her
And it drove him insane,
Because he couldn't reach her.
And embrace the beauty,
Who found the courage,
To move on,
Leaving him crushed,
By the weight of regret.
Words couldn't fill the divide,
Nor reason,
As he moved heaven and earth,
Just to taste her lips again.
Feel her heart beating next to his.
The memory of her form,
Has faded from his mind,
Like her touch,
Only her voice remains,

Twisted among the chorus,
Of echoes inside his head.

❖ ❖ ❖

Everything hurts
Aches,
And my heart is breaking.
You broke through my bones,
To clinch my heart in your hands.
Morbid laced bones,
Used to crisscross,
My heart.
Bloody hands,
Red lipstick and pain,
Trailed across my chest,
As you ripped my muscle,
From its cage,
Setting the monster free,
With your touch.
Letting my heart dream,
Of a phantom love,
You left swinging,
From the gallows,
Tied with laced.

❖ ❖ ❖

The years **burn away**
Like a candle's flickering flame,
These unbreakable strings,
Still connect us,
Even though,
You're gone from the world.

❖ ❖ ❖

Unbreakable strings
Laced together,
Interlocking,
At the heart,
Between us.
All you have to do,
Is smile,
And a song,
Plays from those cords.

It's okay
I'll play the villain,
And turn my cloak,
So, don't piss and moan,
When I do you wrong,
And burn your world,
When I value my peace,
Or rip apart existence,
For her love.
I'll go down swinging,
Fighting,
For every breathe,
To savor her perfume,
And the flavor of her kiss.

The storms in my head
Make me cringe inside.
Because I don't know,
What is a lie,
Or bent truth,
You try to pass along as real.

Spinning your wheels,
Trying to make me understand,
Your lines,
And your rhymes,
Questioning reality,
Whether I should love you,
Or not.
By your actions you left me alone,
Adrift on an island.
A misguided paradise,
Made for someone like me,
Lost in heartache of a person,
Drowning at sea.

Rusted chains
Brittle and break,
After wearing away,
The lock without a key.
Every link,
Hung around my neck,
Attached to a cage,
Where my heart lives.
An untamed beast,
Lurking in the shadows,
Wanting to be free,
And love again.
Roam the alleys,
And highways,
For a beauty,
To die for.
But I have to let go,
Of you,
Of me,
And let it end with me.

❖ ❖ ❖

Her lips
Taste like autumn,
Of S'mores,
And chilly nights,
Wrapped up in blankets,
By a bonfire.
Curled up,
Next to you,
With dancing flames,
And twinkling stars,
Reflected in the prism,
Of your eyes.
She tastes like chaos,
And Christmas,
Hot chocolate,
Fantasies of sugar plums,
Of childhood dreams,
And innocence of life.
Her kiss,
Tastes like heaven,
Of home,
Of memories,
And things,
I once held,
In my arms,
Like she holds me.

❖ ❖ ❖

Winter's chill captivates me,
Sending shivers all over my body.
Cold hands, warm heart,
She says with a smile,

Before kissing my cheek.
Winter's rainbow dances,
Into view over our heads.
Aurora Borealis,
She said with a gasp,
As blueish green ribbons,
Reach across the sky.
Out twinkling the stars,
It seemed at times.
Even the moon was,
Hesitant stay,
As it fled the night,
For the horizon.
Fingers weaved into mine,
When she wrapped my arms,
Around her body.
"It's so beautiful," she said.
"So, is this moment with you," I said.
Before I dropped to one knee,
With a ring in my hand,
And winter's rainbow,
Flowing like a river,
I asked her to be mine.

Her kisses
Taste like sunshine,
And rain in summer.
Cold, and refreshing,
Upon your skin,
And soothing to your soul.
She'll make you shiver,
From her kiss.

She broke the mirror
And cradled her face,
In the palms of her hands,
As tears gathered in her palms.
A shattered mirror for a pretty face,
It was all a pipe dream,
That exploded in her face,
When he broke her heart.

❖ ❖ ❖

Hope whispers
While you sleep,
To the angels,
Up on high.
It speaks to them,
Hoping,
They will be listening,
As your heart,
Longs to feel,
The touch of an angel.

❖ ❖ ❖

I get drunk on you,
Drunk on poetry,
Of words when I taste them,
As they pour from your lips.
And I find myself,
Wanting more,
With every kiss,
When those words trickle,
Like a fountain of a spring.

❖ ❖ ❖

Spending days in my head,
Searching for an escape,
Pouring over things,
That weigh me down.
It's the frustration,
Of it all,
When you can't turn it off,
Because you want to playthings out,
Always on repeat,
Depleting my energy,
With wasted thoughts,
About my health or family.
It is a constant circle,
Of emotions,
Because I want to fight,
But it's an uphill battle,
All the way,
And doing it alone.

Sparkling eyes,
Twinkle like stars,
Laying close,
In the low light.
Painted memories,
Of your silhouette,
Grace my bedside.
And I got lost,
In the spiral,
Of the stars,
Illuminating your soul.
Those little lights,

Surrounded me,
As I drowned,
In the soft blue sea,
Of your iris.
And I lost in an ocean,
Of blissful imagination,
In a place I called home,
Laying here with the memory,
Of your ghost.

❖ ❖ ❖

I ache to taste your lips
But I don't know you,
I only know the fantasy,
I make you to be,
In my head.
And I long to make,
Love to you,
Build memories of us,
As we fall in love together.
Maybe it's my imagination,
Or wishful thinking,
Hell, you don't even remember my name.
So why do I hold these,
Moments of wanting,
To feel the touch of your hand,
Or feel your embrace,
For longer than a moment.

❖ ❖ ❖

Am I numb
To everything,

Around me.
Where you're,
Running on autopilot,
To get through the day.
Things happen,
And you have no emotion,
To show for all the changes,
That surround it.
It feels like a head long dive,
Into the abyss,
And you wonder,
When you're going to break,
The surface for that gasp,
Of air for your burning lungs.
Trying to find a spark,
Or some form of motivation,
To push through,
When you just want to give up.
But for some reason,
I still find a way to get up.

The walls speak of you,
This place called home,
Is what I felt,
While lying here,
Drawn deep into you.

Happy New Year,
Father time wonders,
The **halls of time**

Walls of clocks,
Shelves,
Lined with hourglasses.
One-by-one,
Winding the clocks,
Rolling forward.
Ticking away the days,
Moments,
Shiny grains of sand,
Slide,
Through the hourglass,
Like sparkling diamonds,
Shimmering in the light.
Sands pour,
From one glass to another,
As the ticking clocks,
Chime ringing in the New Year,
And a new figure,
Winds the clocks,
As the old man,
Turns to sand,
And is encased behind glass.

She is made of glass
And all the sparkling things,
That makes her so fragile,
And he broke her.
If she only knew,
That I would have,
Ruined my hands,
To replace her pieces,
But she threw me away,

For him.
So, I can only watch,
As she scatters herself,
Across the floor,
Trying to pull herself,
Back together alone.

❖ ❖ ❖

Come and find me,
Won't you?
My legs are tired,
I'm weary,
From chasing your ghost,
And watching you,
Slip from my grasp,
Every time I've found you.

❖ ❖ ❖

I painted your silhouette
Upon the walls of my mind.
This is the only place,
Where the memory of us,
Still plays in my head.
I can feel your body,
Pressed against mine,
As the echoes of those sparks,
Shimmer along my cortex,
Of my head space.
Regret rings louder here,
Of all those times,
Where I want to be lost,
In your eyes once more,

Drown in your kisses,
Feel your naked body,
Burning against my own,
In the night.
This is my punishment,
For loving you,
When you could not endure,
A love like mine.

I remember,
Kissing your neck,
Instead of your lips.
Perhaps,
If I kissed you there,
Maybe we would have connected.
I wonder if your lips,
Were as soft,
As your neck,
When I trailed my kisses,
Along your neck,
To your shoulder.
I can still feel you,
Grinding your hips,
Into mine.
I should have taken you,
And ravaged you,
Drinking from your body.
Creating memories,
Of us being intertwined,
In a heap of sex and lust.
Before lying with you,
As we cool from the marathon,

Of pounding flesh.

◆ ◆ ◆

How do I last in the moment,
And **enjoy the things**,
In the middle of it all.
How do I find my joy,
And hold onto it,
Within me.
Do I look deep inside,
To find my happiness,
And rebel there,
Through the lows of life.

◆ ◆ ◆

She's a mystery,
One I want to explore,
And learn her story,
While we dance,
In a lovers embrace.
Is it possible,
For me to look,
Into your eyes,
And know,
That you and I,
Were meant to be.

◆ ◆ ◆

Dreams,
Memories,
All they are.

Stardust dreams,
And in the magic,
Of it all.
We kissed,
Kissed,
And all the noise,
Lighting up my head,
Died away,
As your voice,
Silenced,
The demons,
And they hid,
From the light,
Of your soul,
As it shined,
Through the prism,
Of my iris.

Sometimes I wonder
Why I can't attract love,
Rather than weirdos,
Or run off a woman,
Who don't understand,
The love that I give.
It's frustratingly funny,
As I sit and watch people,
Try to understand me,
Sometimes I can see the wheels,
Turning inside their heads,
In trying to figure out a way,
To manipulate me,
To bend to their will.

I love myself too much,
To destroy myself,
For someone,
That doesn't care about me.

❖ ❖ ❖

Dreams **whatever** may come, or pass is the magic of living.

❖ ❖ ❖

I put a spell on you,
One to bewitch you,
Entangle you in my web,
So, you would be fascinated,
By the beauty of life,
Rather than despair,
And melancholy.

❖ ❖ ❖

Her eyes,
Were made of emeralds,
And shimmered,
When she spoke to me,
"I put a spell on you,"
She said with a smile,
As I tasted her crimson lips.

❖ ❖ ❖

I put a spell on you,
So, you would know,
The **gravity of my love**.

I won't let you waste it,
Waste me,
Or the magic,
When we kissed.

It takes strength,
To wander in the dark,
Alone sometimes.
You learn not to fear the night,
Nor the creatures,
Who dwell there.
It's the only home I know.

Stars wait to dance in the dark,
And wander across the night.
The only courage you have,
To chart the heavens,
Depends on the strength
Of your coffee's caffeine level.

Unspoken words,
Wander through,
My sleepless mind.
I dream poetry,
When I dream of you.
Words with meaning,
Attached to the embers,
Of your kisses.

I dream poetry,
Words,
Lines,
Without form,
Like I draw breath.
Breathing in words,
As they course,
Through my veins,
And flow out my pen.
Words,
I find meaning,
But fail,
When I try to speak to them.
I lost my courage,
In trying to speak,
Because my heart,
Can't take the pain,
Even though,
It's the price of life,
Desiring to be loved.

Waves crash,
Upon a distant shore,
Where you lie,
The sandy beach,
Drinking in the sun.
Copper toned skin,
Laced in postage stamps,
And imaginary thread.
Red locks,
Wash over your shoulders,

Like the tides,
Washing away your form.
Tiny beads of perspiration,
Travel along your body,
Cooling touches,
From the sun.
My memory of that day,
Gazing into the eyes,
Of an angel,
Basking in the sunlight.
Grains of sand,
Cleaning to your body,
Conceal hidden parts.
Letting my mind,
Run wild,
As streaks of water,
Tease me,
As it reveals,
Pieces of you.

◆ ◆ ◆

How did we get this way?
One day we're falling in love,
Then time passes,
And you find yourself,
In the arms of a stranger.
How did this come to pass?
It seemed like we were,
So, much more,
Than a one-night stand.
But here we are,
Once we're lovers,
Now we're nothing,

Things don't click,
Like they used too,
Between us.
All the decisiveness,
Being conceded,
And letting,
The ragged edges,
Sever our heart strings.
I go to bed,
Questioning everything,
I once knew about you.
We used to love each other,
What went wrong?
All the simple things,
I loved about you,
Now annoy me,
And drives us apart,
Like a wedge,
Banging away at our faults.
At the end of the day,
I find myself here,
In the arms of a stranger.

The delicate truth.
Perhaps,
Would've been better,
Then the slow death,
Of watching you,
Walking away,
With my heart,
Drowning in your wake,
And enduring the pain.

Delicate steps,
A dancer's motion,
Slow like a leaf,
Floating,
Across the floor.
She slides,
Heel to toe,
Balancing between twirls,
As she comes to rest,
Gliding into my arms.

◆ ◆ ◆

Empty promises,
Empty vows,
White lies,
And golden truths.
It's all about the games,
We play,
When the truth,
Goes so much further
If you like her.

◆ ◆ ◆

I hung on your every word,
Syllable and chorus,
When you spoke,
Because every line,
Awaken the child,
Hidden in me.
Someone wanted to play,
And gleefully,
My heart sprung to life,
As it rode the roller coaster,

Before it dove into your eyes,
Swimming in the blue of your iris.
The closer I drew into you,
Your voice hesitated,
And I found myself,
Asking,
If there was someone else,
While fighting,
To pull my heartstrings,
In the hopes,
Of rescuing my drowning heart,
Before it is lost forever.
Kicking,
Screaming,
I wrestle my heart,
And cradle it,
Like a child,
Who doesn't understand,
Why it plays alone.

◆ ◆ ◆

Am I meant for something more,
Than being passed over in life?
For all I do,
I'm still being left in the dust,
No matter how much I fight.
What do I have to do?
Sometimes I wish,
I could wipe it all away,
And start over again,
Leaving all of them,
In the destruction of my wake.
Alas, it's worthless to try,
Because they don't know,
The depths of my pain,

And once I'm gone,
They will not remember me,
Nor will they care.

Maybe I'm just unworthy of love,
And all these lines of spoken words,
Are meaningless for someone like me.
Love is **a fool's paradise**,
And I'm standing on the beach,
Watching the waves crash upon the shore.
When all I ever wanted,
To see the world through divine eyes,
Ones made of blue sapphires,
With traces of gold flakes.
A timeless beauty,
Who's elegant form,
Was etched into my memories,
As I rode the waves of a heavenly kiss.
Where I was lost in the stardust,
Of you and every moment,
I grasped with all my might,
To hold onto you,
Before you faded from my fingertips.
I guess I'll long for love,
Till forever dies in the stars.

Maybe I'm just unworthy of love,

"Sip me slow,
Like **a fine wine**," she said.
So, with every breath,
I took her,
Until I was under her spell.
Locked into her eyes,

And in the throes of passion.
"It's a bliss," she said.
Riding her,
Tugging on her hair,
Laced between my fingers.
Were we just a summer affair?
Drifting between the sheets,
Until I drain her cup dry.

What do you do,
When you want,
To touch a beauty.
When your eyes meet,
And in an explosion,
Of stardust.
You see the magic,
Of her soul.
The light,
She pours,
From her touch,
When she reciprocates,
Taking away the madness,
You feel deep within,
Your heart,
Because she takes,
Away the ache,
Of loneliness.

It is maddening,
Trying to make you,
Understand,
Where I am coming.

I overthink it all,
From the time I awake,
To the time my head,
Hits the pillow.
It's a constant,
River of thought,
Streaming through,
My head.
All of it,
Even in silence,
There's thoughts,
Gliding along,
A clear plain of glass,
In my head space.
Memories,
And lies.
Each thought,
Mixed with sadness,
Guilt and feeling numb,
From all the regret,
And you want me,
To pull happy memories,
From the abyss?
I remember things,
As they play like a movie,
35mm film winds,
Around the reel,
As the light,
Burns them,
Into the walls,
Of my skull.
No sound,
Only ghost,
Shimmering,
Across a screen,
Of light.

Faces,
Etched into my heart,
As tears fall.

She dances across the sky,
And with each **passing night**,
She slowly reveals her body,
For all eyes to see.
She longs to held,
In the arms of her lover,
As they rarely share the sky,
Together in the daytime.
The sun bathes the moon,
In sunlight,
As her silhouette twirls,
Upon a back lit canopy.
Naked she drifts,
Among the stars and stardust,
Hiding her figure behind a cloud,
Just to play coy when her lover,
Is around.

I carry a box of memories,
Where all the **words of my heart**,
Are written upon these pages.
Not a single page is blank,
They are all stained,
With my blood and tears,
Bound together by my heart strings,
And as I turn the pages,
A song plays.
One for every chapter,

Bittersweet at times,
Stirring melodies,
Transcend time,
To help tell the story of me.
Every line,
Every verse,
Had the sweetest sound,
Before it was drowned out,
When the curtain fell,
The act moved onto the next.
There are more stories to tell,
As I add more notes,
To the pages of notebooks.

Roses are red,
And **your vines**,
Entangle me,
Gripping thrones,
Draw me in,
Tearing my flesh,
As I try to escape,
Your grasp.
You weave your spell,
Leaving me enchanted,
By your fragrance,
Of madness,
And sexual desire.
I can't escape the attraction,
Of a femme fatal.
An old flame,
Becomes rekindled,
And I fall into slavery,

143

Of your sex,
On Valentine's Day.

◆ ◆ ◆

All cloud tops,
Memories,
Wondering through,
Daydreams,
And relaxing,
On gentle winds.

◆ ◆ ◆

Let go,
And find your courage man.
She's human like you.
Beautiful,
Enchanting and elegant.
Why is it so hard.
She's probably married,
Has a boyfriend,
Or a girlfriend.
So do I bite the bullet,
And cling to her in friendship,
Just to die inside,
When she is right there,
Slipping through my fingers,
Every second of my life.
Are you worth the pain?
The voices in my head ask,
While on repeat,
So their words echo,
Inside my mind.
All my courage is spent,
It seems like,

I'm just spinning my wheels,
In place as everything else,
Flies by me.

◆ ◆ ◆

Lost **in the haze**,
Of memories.
I struggle,
To clear the cobwebs.
My body aches for your touch,
And all I can do,
Is remember the sound,
Of your voice echoing in my head.

◆ ◆ ◆

Make a wish upon me,
Blow with a deep breath,
To scatter my seeds,
Far and wide.
Let me take your wishes,
All your dreams,
And sadness a way.
I will carry them,
Beyond the hills,
And valleys,
Across rivers and streams.
Let me,
Plant my seeds,
Before you step here,
So you too,
Will rise from the ground,
In a new place.

◆ ◆ ◆

Lines are drawn in the sand,
Being tired of running,
I choose to stand my ground.
One of us is going down,
One of us is leaving,
And I choose violence,
Because we were done,
A long time ago.

◆ ◆ ◆

For a change,
It's another page,
That needs to be turned,
Maybe it will be easy,
Changing for something more,
More than this.
Waking up to an empty room,
Being chased by shadows,
From your past,
All for kindness sake.
It's a struggle,
Wanting something more,
And feeling yourself slipping away.

◆ ◆ ◆

I feel your **touch upon my face**,
A phantom feeling of you,
Straddling me as your run your fingers,
Through my hair,
Cupping my face,
In the palm of your hand,
Before we kiss.
I trace my fingers along your back,
And feel the warmth of an angel,

Black wings fan out,
As you wrap them around us,
Sheltering us the world.
We kiss again,
And again,
As I fall deeper into you.

♦ ♦ ♦

Painted lines,
Of **simple things**,
Next to you,
Tracing shapes,
In your palm,
As we drift asleep.
This is where I want to be.
Your head on my shoulder,
Wrapped up in my arms.
Making love,
To woman I adore,
Nothing can compare.
Feeling blue,
When I'm lost in you,
Is the only place,
I'd rather be.
Lost in the moment,
Of creating a memory,
With you.

ABCDE finally getting over you,
Long after you've been gone.
Hoping I'll find a way,
To **heal all my scars**.
Just letting go of my hate,

Knowing we shared the blame.
Losing all control,
As my world starts to spin,
Crazy as it seems,
I feel so alive,
Without you being here.
So, go out with your friends,
Sleep whomever you want,
I won't be around,
When you fall down.
Go find some friends,
To wipe away,
Beer-stained tears.

◆ ◆ ◆

Tracing your face,
And **remembering**,
Everything,
About your face.
Your dimples,
Soft lips,
And freckles,
Scattered like stars,
On a moonless night,
Across your cheeks.
Warm eyes,
Peering,
From the shadows,
Beneath golden strands.
Long, deep kisses.
Getting lost,
In how you taste,
So I won't forget,
The woman,
I call mine.

Lacing my fingers,
Between yours,
And making shapes,
In the palm of your hand.
Not wanting to lose,
These moments,
To the sands of time.

◆ ◆ ◆

There was a time when you wanted them,
Those words, and lines,
Only with a hyphenated name,
But you wanted it.
I guess you felt with my name,
I laid claim to you,
When I never tried to imprison you,
Those weren't my intentions.
You were always free,
To be the person,
I fell in love with.
So you didn't want my name,
Nor my hand,
My heart,
You didn't have rip it,
From my heart strings.
I gave it freely to you,
With every breath I took.
You took his name,
Or maybe hers,
I hope you find happiness,
Because you couldn't find it,
Here with me.

◆ ◆ ◆

Let's get drunk on each other,
And **stagger off to bed**,
Somewhere between the sheets,
And explore each other's scars.
Trace them with our fingers,
While kissing them softly.

Draw me **into your flames**,
Because I want to burn with you.
Like a wick of a candle,
I'm drawn to you,
The feel of your skin,
Burning me with every touch,
As you consume me.
Lost in the inferno,
Your hair blazes,
Like the flames,
Dancing round us,
pouring over us like a tide.
We were meant to explode,
And be a washed in our light,
Of two souls burning in love.
Burning away,
My fears,
All my logic,
So a new man,
Rises from the ashes,
To meet the kiss of a phoenix.

❖ ❖ ❖

The feel of you,

Is my addiction,
Because holding you,
Was the closest,
I've been to being home.
So here I am,
Being powerless,
In not knowing,
What I should do,
To win your heart,
Or even if I am worthy,
To be your man.
What can I do,
I get lost in your eyes,
Every time,
I look into them,
And wonder,
If you feel the same way.

Old pages,
Torn edges,
Where dreams,
Are stains,
Between the lines.
Here and there,
Old rhymes,
Where old songs,
Carry tunes,
Of memories.
The phrases,
Remain the same,
Though my love,
For you never dies,
And the echoes,
Of long dried ink,

Still call out your name.

❖ ❖ ❖

It feels like,
You are **out of my reach**.
A ghost who haunts my dreams,
And I wake to your memory.
I am so tired,
And weary from all of this waiting,
Waiting for you to walk into my life.
I don't have the desire anymore,
Because it has burned me out.
Snuffed out like candle,
Beneath a shot glass.
I'm too old and my days are short,
And I'm trying to survive.
It's the only thing I know,
Since you've never been here,
In these arms.

❖ ❖ ❖

I want to dance,
By the shore of **your iris**,
And test the waters,
With the touch of my fingers.
Watch the ripples,
Sparkle in your eyes.

❖ ❖ ❖

All the pieces of me,
You gathered me into your arms,

Every **shard, and fragile sliver**.
You took your time,
Weaving them together,
With the touch of your fingers,
You forged with love.
All those shards,
Tied with heart strings,
Duct tape, and glue.
Wrapped in a bandage,
As you guided me,
From my knees,
To my feet,
With a tender kiss.

◆ ◆ ◆

Broken man
Beneath this skin,
Lies a fractured human.
After the angel was set free,
From the stone,
By the hammer and chisel,
Of the artist's hand.
Flaws developed,
Cracks,
Malformed the shape,
Of this person.
Me.
I'm damaged,
From all the trauma,
I've endured over the years.
I'm not perfect,
Yet,
I am supposed to be.
As a man,
I'm not supposed to feel,

Or care,
Just sacrifice myself,
Out of silent pain,
And longing,
For something,
That's a fairy tale.
Show no emotions,
No concern,
Feel nothing,
But cold stone,
Of my flesh.
Everything is bland,
Because my senses,
Are broken,
Along with my mind.
The chemicals,
Wash away the feeling,
Of euphoria,
When there's nothing,
To mend these broken pieces,
Between my mind,
And body.
My thoughts,
Don't matter,
Because all the avenues,
Where I once spoke,
Have been long forgotten,
Or those people are gone.
You battle depression,
And the guilt of overthinking,
Replaying the past,
To change the outcome of things.
Trying to rewrite,
Every loss into a victory.
Then the overthinking,
Lends itself to madness,

As your anxiety,
Peaks from the wonder,
Of the future.
Even though you tell yourself,
The future is bright,
Only you focus,
On the dark corners,
Wondering,
What will come,
From those places.
Then it is the longing,
To feel the touch,
Of a woman again.
The taste of her skin,
And the joy,
Of exploring,
Places of her body,
Which my mind,
Has a difficult time,
Remembering,
The sensation,
Of texture,
Of her body parts,
Under my touch.
The feeling of her aura,
And the energy,
You exchanged,
In the moment of passion,
Or just sexual release.
Even sex,
Has no meaning,
When you draw down,
The basics of things.
It's only masturbation,
With another body.
Only the chemicals,

Make it out to be love.
All those years,
Turned my traumas,
Into a wall,
That I fail to overcome,
And I've yet, met a woman,
Willing to scale it,
Seeking a broken man behind them.

◆ ◆ ◆

Crumbled **beneath the covers**,
Pulling closer to you.
So, I can drown,
In your morning whispers,
Caught somewhere,
Between a dream
And careless thoughts.

◆ ◆ ◆

Follow the lines,
Like the **beating of a heart**.
Tangled up in you,
And I only want to dream.
Because it is only place,
I have found,
Where I can physically touch you,
And hold a ghost,
Even it was only for a night.
It's a magical moment,
Sharing a space,
Where our minds,
Can connect.
I hunger to feel the heat of you,
Wrapped up in my arms.

◆ ◆ ◆

It's complicated,
All the situations,
You find yourself,
Often fighting for.
Love, friendships, and family.
All not in that order,
Because every breath,
Is spent on healing wounds,
Finding peace,
Or wasting away,
Trying to figure out,
What to do with your life.
The frustration of it all,
And you can't win.
But you have to fight,
Because sinking,
Isn't an option.
No matter how the water,
Rushes to cover you,
Beneath the waves,
Of uncertainty.
It's a familiar friend,
The one you wish,
You didn't know.
So, hello uncertainty,
At least you're not draped,
In a cloak of depression,
With the mask of anxiety.

Reflections of you and I,
Lost somewhere,

In-between the noise of life.
I've watched you leave,
So many times,
No matter what form you took,
Tall, short, fat or thin.
Brown,
Blonde,
Red,
Or raven haired beauties.
The revolving door,
Still turns like a record,
Playing a familiar song.
Your song,
And I remember every note,
Every line, and time,
I cried between the verses,
Being lost without you.
No matter how much,
I work to let you go,
Every heartbeat,
Recalls your voice,
And my mind goes wild,
As I hallucinate,
Seeing your silhouette,
Everywhere I turn.
Imagining your still here,
Curled up next me,
Alone in the dark.
The faint scent of you,
Still lingers on the pillows,
And pieces of your hairs,
Found their way,
Woven into my clothes,
Like the knots,
My heart has been tied into,
The day you just walked away.

Even though It was me,
Who pushed you a way.

Her eyes changed,
From **blue to violet**,
When the sun set.
Sprinkled with little lights,
Like the starry night.
And from that moment,
I was lost in a violet haze.

Thinking of you,
What a dream,
To hold you in my arms.
Listen to you,
Whisper my name,
When we're alone.
I just want,
To spend forever,
With you.
Not out of loneliness,
But love.
And gaze into your eyes,
So deep,
All the riddles of the universe,
Reveal themselves,
Written upon your soul.

Colors of a new day,
Breaking through,

The gloom of night.
Shadows,
Have nowhere to hide,
As they reveal their secrets,
To the light of day.
Black and white,
Become purple, blues and gold.
Red hues, and orange.
Change the night,
Blankets the stars,
And shrouds the moon,
In a pale blue reef.
Slow clouds,
Paint the dawn,
With a dazzling display,
Of life being renewed.

My hope was gone,
Just another **burned romance**,
With the ashes scattered,
Among the ruins of love.
How could this be?
One more flame,
Another candle flickers,
As I watch it burn,
And wish I could,
Hold onto you for a moment.
Because love was gone in a flash.

Caught up
Revolving around the Earth,
Another day,

One more turn,
Maybe things will be different.
Perhaps my love would be strong enough,
Or I would be enough to push away the shadows.
Another pretty face,
And a reason to find the solution,
At the bottom of a bottle.
She doesn't see,
How beautiful she is in my eyes.
Where you dream,
Or day dream about waking up,
Next to a goddess.
Countless dreams,
All burn in the morning light.
Like nightmares,
Melting in the webs of a dream catcher.
Just for a moment,
Or a night,
Just to hold her,
Here in my arms,
For one more day,
Passes me by.
Trying to find the courage,
To tell her how I feel.
Three simple words,
That get lost in my throat.
I found myself drowning in her smile,
Trying to swim against the currents,
Of the shifting tides,
Hidden within my head,
Because I'm all caught up in you.

◆ ◆ ◆

I was sleepwalking.
Happy in my slumber,

With my **deep dreaming bliss**.
And with the touch of your hand,
You woke me from a dream.
Ever since then,
I've been living,
In a nightmare existence,
Without you.
I should have kissed you,
Something simple,
Perhaps,
I would have fallen,
Back to sleep,
And continue dreaming,
Of a world in ignorance.

◆ ◆ ◆

I used to be someone you loved,
The person you once knew.
I was your knight in shining armor,
What was it,
That changed between us?
Am I not the same man you knew?
Beneath my skin,
To where this heartbeats?
What changed for you,
To see me in a different light?
I'm not perfect,
Nor did I ever claim to be.
You got mad because I challenged you,
On the things you thought were real.
I am not responsible for the image,
Your mind creates of me.
I wanted a life like you - with you.
Something more.

However, over time you thought,
I could fit into you square circled hole,
You tried to pigeon-hole me into.
You know that's not me,
Like it wasn't you,
But there we were.
I was a fool to think,
Love would conquer all,
And I overlooked,
Your imperfections,
All your mistakes.
Only you were the one,
Secretly holding a list,
Of all the wrongs I did.
Because you've been searching,
For an out since the beginning,
And this was your chance.
Making me the person you used to love,
Just a stranger,
Sleeping next to you in the dark,
While you dreamed of someone else.
Another knight in shining armor,
To win the day,
From the person you used to love.

◆ ◆ ◆

Kisses,
Wishes,
And dimples.
Dreams,
Of madness,
Without crazy.
It's an ocean,
And some people,
Drown while,

Standing on the shore.
They swim in the shallows,
Barely above their ankles,
Yet, they tell you about stories,
About the vast rivers,
They have crossed,
To only find nothing,
Waiting for them on the other side.

◆ ◆ ◆

White lace,
And trim.
All the things,
Pure as snow.
Winter kisses.
Is this a fantasy,
To look into your eyes,
And see something,
Magnificent to behold.

◆ ◆ ◆

Searching for hope again,
Because something happened,
Where I lost the fire,
Of being me.
My wings are not clipped,
I keep telling myself.
So why can't I fly?
What grounded me?
Losing everything,
That I held dear,
Was the nail in the coffin,
But I live and that is my choice.
I desire to write,

Only I stare at a blank screen,
As a cursor flashes upon the screen.
Books don't write themselves,
Nor do pages sprout ink.
No music or rhymes,
Move my needle to inspire me.

◆ ◆ ◆

Drifting on a cascade of merriment - **along the way.**
Somewhere between a fantasy,
And a dream.
That's where I find you.
I've become lost in my head,
Because holding you,
Is something of a mystery,
That I long to solve.
Knowing how you feel,
Wrapped up in my arms.
I can't reason,
Or grasp how a woman feels,
Because I have lost the imagination,
To recall the brilliant sensation,
Of tracing your silhouette,
Beneath my fingers.
All the pieces of her,
I want to feel.
Even if it was just for a mire moment,
That we touched,
In some form or another.
Whether it was a brush of your hand.
Mine upon your leg.
The feel of your hugs,
Because my soul aches,
To read the words,
Written beneath your skin,

When your goose bumps rise.

Do you know how hard it is,
Trying to not think about things,
When you're **on the road**?
Deep down,
You think about life,
And how the minutes tick away.
When you're alone in your head,
For hours,
You dwell on things.
Life and death.
All the complexity of it,
While concentrating on everything else,
Going on around you.
Because you think about people,
Places, things.
Your past, present, and future.
And all the anxiety, and depression,
That comes with the wonder of it all.
Not the where did I go wrong,
Nor how did I get here,
Only what do I do from here?
Existing beyond things.
Your imagination plays around,
With all the thoughts you have,
And they run through your head,
Like a freight train hell bent,
On reaching the next station.
I often wonder what it would be like,
To meet someone,
Date someone again.
Then a voice inside your head,
Says to you: "Do you have time left?"

You're not getting any younger,
Kids are becoming a faded dream,
Because the older you get,
The less time you will have,
Being a part of their lives.
You wonder,
Where can I afford a house,
A life,
As you try to rub two cents together,
To make a living.
It's even worse,
When you have a bad day.
You replay the events,
That triggered you,
Making you angrier,
By the mile.
You close your eyes,
And hope there's enough time,
Left with your body,
To accomplish what dreams,
Remain inside your heart.

She held me close,
Whispering to me.
Faint words,
She spoke,
About love.
Words shared,
Between two lovers.
It was bliss,
Holding her.
"Say you love me."
She said softly.
I got carried away,

When I told her,
I was madly in love,
With a woman,
Who is the brightest light,
Shining in the darkness,
Of my hollow shell of a heart,
And her light,
Chased away my demons,
While quenching my spirit,
With her kisses.

She chased golden butterflies,
Landing **on lilac tulips**.
Only to watch them take flight,
Dancing in the summer sun.
It was magic to her,
Watching them climb higher,
For a blonde headed girl,
Twirling in the sunshine,
Wishing she could fly.
She laughed,
And sung to the butterflies.
As they drifted closer,
Only to remain out of reach.
She didn't care,
"They were beautiful," she said.
As she lay on the ground,
Watching them float above her.
Lost in the moment of being young.

I wonder what it would be like,
To taste you,

A bittersweet feeling,
Every time we touch.
I get lost in the way you glide,
Across the room.
It's an elegant fantasy,
Imagining you coming towards me,
As we sink into the bed.
I dream of waking up beside you,
And letting my fingers,
Feel the heat of your skin.
Tracing your form,
Exploring the beauty.
You're body isn't mine,
But there are times,
When I want to be the one,
You hold tightly in the night,
When the darkness comes,
To capture you.
Soft kisses,
And the mysteries your body possesses,
I desire to unlock them,
As you discover mine.
All the ones written upon your skin,
And the rest buried beneath.
I want to know your mind,
And all the things,
That make you.
All the darkness,
Rage and pain.
Happiness, and dreams.
All the things you tell yourself,
To help you make it through your day,
When I'm not there to snuggle you,
In my arms.

There's no combination,
To **unlock these chains**,
Because I am chained to you.
Your memory,
Haunts my dreams,
And you rattle those chains,
Every time my mind,
Remembers you.
Every link of the chain,
A time we shared,
Between locks,
And the broken pieces,
Of metal strung together,
By the forces of nature,
We were too young to comprehend.
Every link,
Was something that bonded us together.
And I spend many nights,
Counting those links of memory,
Like seconds on the clock,
Of how I loved you with all my heart.
I know you wouldn't want this,
Being tied to your memory,
With a chain,
And drowning in your lost love.

She's the substance,
I desire to abuse.
Coursing through my veins,
Lingering on my brain.
She's all I want,
Just to feel numb.
Somehow,

I get lost along the way.
There's so much,
In-between the rise,
And fall of the high.
I am on when you're near,
So, I ride along the waves,
Of your words,
The moment they slide,
From your soft lips.
Because a drug like you,
Is ecstasy,
Being submerged in you.
Your legs are a dream,
I want wrapped around me,
Tightly just to be connected,
To the source,
Of my addiction.
It is possible to drown,
In the madness,
Your body creates,
When I gaze upon,
A goddess,
Whose freedom,
From the stone,
Which you were carved,
Makes me wish,
I could possess,
A piece of you,
Since,
You're beyond my touch.

Sparkling jewels,

Shimmer along the surface.
Deep or shallow,
They move with the wind,
Across a smooth plain of glass.
Silver lights,
Gleaming in the sun's delight,
Casting reflections back to the stars.
Diamonds crash,
Upon the water's edge.
Exposing rock by washing away dust,
Dulling the rough surface of jewels.

Laced satin
Wrapped,
Reefed,
With a yellow center.
Delicate petals,
But strong enough,
To hold,
Or cradle a bumblebee,
As they caress each other,
In an embrace.

Little **space in white**
Matches your dress.
All the things,
One can imagine.
I met you here,
Asked for your hand there,
And we said our vows,
Beneath the halo.
It was a beautiful day,

A radiant dream,
As your amber eyes,
Glowed with delight.
It was our day,
Surrounded by our friends,
Lost in the moment,
Being lost in your kiss,
As we say forever.

◆ ◆ ◆

I'm going out of my mind,
Because that is where you are,
And I am not.
I desire to know your mind,
Yet, I don't know how to ask.
What kind of thoughts,
Resides behind your amber eyes.
I would like to know,
What you think about?
Your deepest thoughts,
Where your mind wonders,
To certain dreams or things.
As I fear it might contain,
A world without me.

◆ ◆ ◆

I don't want to endure this,
Being **sucked into you**.
But every time,
I see your eyes,
Looking back at me,
I feel myself being pulled in,
By your amber pearls.

I become lost in you,
And how you twirl,
And play with your hair,
It frames your silhouette,
So perfectly in my mind,
That it is the only thing,
I find myself thinking about,
Every time I wake up,
Or when I fall asleep.
I'm on a roller coaster,
Riding along the curves,
Of your body,
And I can't let go,
Of the longing I feel,
In wanting to touch you.
No, I desire to kiss your lips,
And taste what heaven is like,
From the lips of an angel.
The memory of you,
Is etched into my mind,
And all I can do is marvel,
At the beauty,
You possess,
Since I am trapped here,
In my head,
Locked away in place,
Where I'm going mad,
Longing to hear you,
Say my name,
And for you,
To call me yours.

❖ ❖ ❖

Another day,
And I am greeted,
By a smiling face,
Lying next to me.
We dressed,
And strolled,
To the back porch.
The smell of coffee,
Roses and you.
I pull you close.
We stare,
At the horizon of love.
Streaks of light,
Broke thru clouds,
Rising,
Above the mountain.
Laced fingers,
Sharing a memory,
Just being lost in you,
For a day.

We met,
Criss-crossed fates,
Of two people.
At two different ends,
Finally bonding,
In a squash of emotions.
We never touched,
But the silence,
Echoing in my sinking soul,
Ached with every breath,

As I longed to hold you.
Every second,
I felt you,
Slipping from my grasp,
And I had no choice,
Only to let you go.

◆ ◆ ◆

I'm **at war** with myself,
Because I want you.
And I can't have you,
It's an endless circle,
I keep finding myself,
In the middle of.
Going around and around,
And I don't know what to do,
To break this cycle,
Of wanting you.
I'm in love with an angel,
And she remains,
At arm's length.
I'm still trapped here,
And I can't let go,
Of you,
So here I am,
Wanting to be free of you.
It seems like an endless circle,
When I come into contact,
With some woman.
I become possessed by her,
So much so,
My mind gets lost,
As my heart finds another folly,

To chase after.
Maybe I'll find a woman,
Who will release me from my prison.
Yet, I find one more pretender,
Dragging me down,
And I'm drowning,
In the fear of losing myself.
After all I've done,
To love myself,
And endure the pain,
Of loving someone,
Who doesn't want to be there,
Doesn't desire you.
I've took that leap,
So many times,
Only to look back,
To see her waving goodbye,
While wrapped,
In another man's arms.
Life crashes over me,
Like the waves,
Pounding upon the shore.
How can you have courage,
When you expect,
Romance to die,
Even before,
It takes flight.
So, here I am,
Waging war within myself,
Hoping that someday,
The caged animal inside me,
Can wonder free,
Without terrorizing my soul.

◆ ◆ ◆

All those simple words,
We used to say.
Tender feelings,
Of expressions,
Where you and I,
Found a connection,
Beyond all the static,
Of life's chaos.
Words intertwined,
The syllables,
Had their own meaning,
Sort of our secret language,
I felt beneath your skin,
With every touch,
When words weren't enough,
Only you and I knew,
And understood.
That was our moment,
Clinging to what we knew,
Because we were so much more,
Then friends.
We knew how each other tasted,
In the throes of passion,
When we burned,
Like a fire,
Melting into each other.

You shiver,
In the **throes**,
Of winter,

Beneath the ocean,
Of you from my touch.
And I get lost,
In the way you feel,
As we exchange,
Stardust from the connection,
Of our souls entangled,
In our embrace.

◆ ◆ ◆

There were so many chapters,
To the **book we write**,
When you and I make love.
Every page of you,
I turn as I write,
My tender kisses,
Along your spine.
I love reading you,
Word for word,
Along those lines,
Where fiction,
Fantasy and reality,
Blur into a beauty,
I love feeling,
Beneath my fingers,
Every time,
I draw you closer to me.
Letting you,
Enter my heart,
As your fingers,
Write your love story,
On the journal,
Of life,
Beating in my chest.

◆ ◆ ◆

How do we turn,
The **chapters of tomorrow**,
When every page,
Is a tearstained ledger,
Of broken hearts and sorrows,
Between two estranged lovers.
It wasn't this way,
Torn apart and lost,
Between the pages,
Of disdain,
And lies.
Love was so new,
But fragile,
And we slowly,
Chipped away,
Scaring the edges,
Of something,
That was a treasure.
Words caused cracks,
Actions broke away the shards,
Until hearts broke,
And tore away,
From the heart strings,
That held us bound,
To each other.
Stretching the fabric,
Of our beings,
Leaving us broken pieces,
And discarded humans.

◆ ◆ ◆

Blue is her name,

She was named,
For the color of her eyes,
And she was beautiful.
She was winter,
Beneath the ocean.
Because her heart,
Was deep as the ocean,
And knew no boundaries,
When she shared her soul.

Don't let me drown,
As I dive **beneath the surface**,
Of the depths of you.
Help me breath,
As we exchange,
Precious air between,
Our kisses.
Drowning in the pools,
Of your brown iris,
Slipping into the black,
As I find myself lost,
In the soul of a beauty,
Whose smile,
Shattered my armor.
All I can do is drown,
In the tangle,
Of your amber locks.

What lies,
Beneath your armor,
That you hide,
From the world?

Perhaps it is lies,
Strung together,
By **your heart strings**.
Tied to a lie,
Intertwined,
With my heart,
And a smile.
You broke,
The boundaries,
That tied us together.
With every breath,
Of a daisy chain,
Laced in the solace,
Of my loneliness.
As you close the door,
On my love,
With another lie.

It's a flood,
These **tides of emotions**,
That wash over me.
Trapped in the ocean of you,
I drown in the madness,
Of your beauty,
As I swim in the cosmos,
Of the spiraling galaxy,
In your soul.
You pull me back to you like gravity,
As my life winds like clock,
Turning me back to you.
I can't let go,
Of the woman,
Who haunts my mind,
And laced my brain,

With the chemicals,
Of my addiction,
When we kiss,
Because you are the only thing,
I want to hold.

◆ ◆ ◆

I wasn't searching for you,
Until you came into my life,
And turned everything upside down,
With just the **sound of your voice**,
And the gentle touch of your hand.
From that moment on,
I surrendered all I knew about myself,
Just to be near you,
To feel your hand in mine,
See your smile,
And be lost with you standing beside me,
A partner in mischief and folly,
Because I fell in love,
With a wayward piece of myself,
I never knew existed.
I was floored by your simple beauty,
So much so my mind wrote poetry,
About the vision of a woman,
Who stood before me.
I was in shock,
When I laid eyes upon you,
And the way the curves of your body,
Lingered to the dance your garments,
Made as they framed your silhouette,
Like the moon paints the edges,
Between light and shadows.
I was mesmerized,
So long before your fingers,

Intertwined into mine,
And I was able to quench my thirst,
With the taste of your lips,
When we embraced for one long kiss.

◆ ◆ ◆

Worlds burn,
Collide,
And here we are.
If I'm **such a dreamer**...
Then why can't I sleep?
Even with you,
Here in my arms,
Wasting, saving time.
As everything,
Comes to an end,
But for this moment,
A glorious kiss.
And I am lost in the moment,
Of everything here,
Wrapped up in my arms,
Because you are everything,
And the reason,
I can't sleep.

Do you know what you are?
Words.
Simple but elegant words,
With curves.
Words with meaning,
Expressed through,
Skin, and scent.

Those of sentences,
That go on forever,
Like the length of your legs,
Down to your toes.
Damning words,
Etched into my head space,
With every step,
My mind creates,
New meaning,
To my imagination,
As I ache,
To feel your naked skin,
Against mine.
So, I can stare into those,
Amber eyes,
At the cosmic tangle,
Of lights hidden in your soul.

Worlds burn,
Collide,
And here we are.
If I'm such a dreamer…
Then **why can't I sleep**?
Even with you,
Here in my arms,
Wasting, saving time.
As everything,
Comes to an end,
But for this moment,
A glorious kiss.
And I am lost in the moment,
Of everything here,

Wrapped up in my arms,
Because you are everything,
And the reason,
I can't sleep.
Is you,
Only you as the imagine of you,
Moves through my head,
Like clouds on a summer day,
Blocking out the sun,
And you block my reasoning,
For wanting to be with you,
Even when I know,
We aren't perfect,
Only enough,
For to broken souls,
Trying to change,
When the rising tide,
Surrounds us.

◆ ◆ ◆

The heart doesn't know forgetting,
Yet, it knows the **pain of letting go**,
Of being torn from the pages of love.
A heart remembers all the moments,
Mixed with memories of things,
It once knew as love.
And it remembers like any muscle,
Even when it's not in use.
The heart knows those feelings,
And tries to remedy,
The emptiness love once filled,
With the memories,
Of a kiss,
A touch,

A lingering scent,
Or causes the mind,
To see images of her face,
On every woman,
You see in the world.
The heart doesn't forget,
And it will remind you,
Of all the pain.

Made in the USA
Columbia, SC
06 June 2022